30 Bicycle Tours in New Hampshire

A Guide to Selected Backcountry Roads throughout the Granite State

Adolphe Bernotas and Tom and Susan Heavey

Third Edition, Revised and Expanded

A 30 Bicycle Tours™ Book

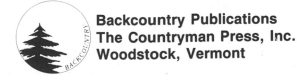
Backcountry Publications
The Countryman Press, Inc.
Woodstock, Vermont

Published by Backcountry Publications
A division of the Countryman Press, Inc.
Woodstock, Vermont 05091

Library of Congress Cataloging-in-Publication Data
Bernotas, Adolphe.
   30 bicycle tours in New Hampshire : a guide to selected
backcountry roads throughout the Granite State / Adolphe Bernotas
and Tom and Susan Heavey. — 3rd ed., rev. and expanded.
     — p.   cm. — (A 30 bicycle tours book)
   Rev. ed. of: 25 bicycle tours in New Hampshire / Tom and Susan
Heavey. Rev. and expanded ed. c1985.
     — ISBN 0-88150-192-1
     — 1. Bicycle touring — New Hampshire — Guide-books.   2. New Hampshire —
Description and travel — 1981 — Guide-books.   I. Heavey, Tom.
II. Heavey, Susan.   III. Heavey, Tom. 25 bicycle tours in New
Hampshire.   IV. Title.   V. Title: Thirty bicycle tours in New
Hampshire.   VI. Series.
GV1045.5.N4H4   1991
917.42′0443 — dc20   91-7546
                                                                        CIP

Typesetting by The Sant Bani Press, Inc.
Text and cover design by Richard Widhu
Maps by Richard Widhu, © 1991 Backcountry Publications
Cover photos, from top to bottom: Bill Finney/NH Office of Vacation Travel; Laura Dore/NH Office of Vacation Travel; Fred McLaughlin/Haggett's Bike Shop, Concord.

Printed in the United States of America
Printed on recycled paper

We wish to dedicate this book to Barbara Leedham and to all those who bicycle on New Hampshire's byways.

Acknowledgments

We want to thank Mary Kibling, Philomena and Ralph Barbieri, Sally Morgan, Seth Bareiss, George Issa, Ted Mitchell, Paul Thomas, Doina Chiacu, John Harrigan, Martha McGannon, Meg Dennison, Lynn Rice, Ann Kennard, Valery Mitchell, Jere Daniell, Janet Biehl, Tim Savard, Cynthia Hunt, Patrick Pallatroni, Laura Scheibel, Suanne Yglesias, Louise Kremzner, Sherri Restuccia, Wendy Panarello, and these Granite State Wheelmen — Kathy Lacharite, Fred McLaughlin, Liz Tucci, Jon-Pierre Lasseigne, John Walsh, Paul de Spagna, Barry Cotter, Mickey Burzynski, Bill Hills, Ed Fisher, Linda Gould, and Lorenzo Bandini.

An Invitation to the Reader — Although it is unlikely that the roads and streets you cycle on these tours will change much with time, some road signs, land-marks, and other items may. If you find that changes have occurred on these routes, please let us know, so that we may correct them in future editions. Address all correspondence to:

Editor
30 Bicycle Tours™ Series
Backcountry Publications, Inc.
P.O. Box 175
Woodstock, Vermont 05091

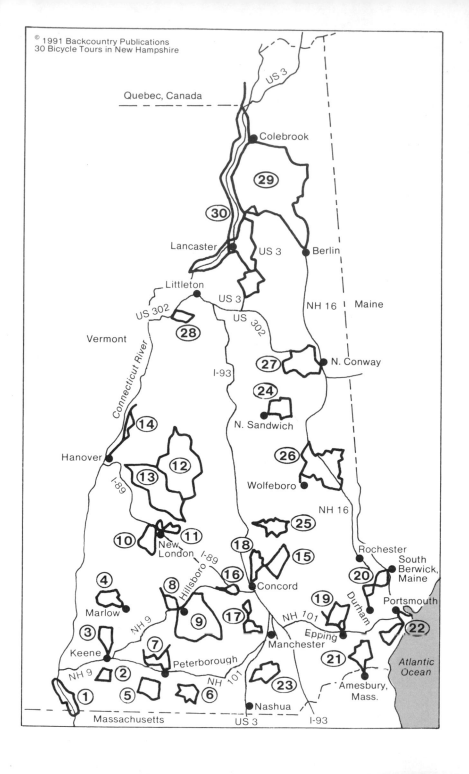

Quebec, Canada

US 3

Colebrook

㉙

㉚

Lancaster

US 3

Berlin

Littleton

US 3

US 302

NH 16

Maine

US 302

Vermont

㉘

I-93

US 302

㉗

N. Conway

㉔

Connecticut River

N. Sandwich

㉖

㉕

㉒

㉓

NH 16

Wolfeboro

㉔

Hanover

I-89

㉓

⑫

⑭

⑬

⑱

⑮

NH 16

Rochester

South
Berwick,
Maine

⑩

⑪

New
London

I-89

⑯

Concord

㉚

Durham

Portsmouth

④

⑧

Hillsboro

⑨

⑰

⑲

NH 101

Epping

㉒

Marlow

③

NH 9

⑦

Peterborough

Manchester

㉑

Atlantic
Ocean

Keene

②

⑤

NH 101

㉓

Amesbury,
Mass.

NH 9

①

⑥

Nashua

Massachusetts

US 3

I-93

Contents

Wellington State Park on Newfound Lake from a viewpoint only a short walk off your route on the Canaan-Newfound Lake tour (see tour 12).

Preface to the Third Edition

In the autumn of 1989, when Susan Heavey, one of the original coauthors of this book, asked me to consider revising *25 Bicycle Tours in New Hampshire,* I was honored and thought it would be a delightful diversion from daily journalism. As I worked on it, it became more than that. The book swallowed up the spring and summer of 1990 in what became a hectic labor of love that gave me an appreciation of the hard work that has been pouring into this book since it was published in 1979, becoming the standard New Hampshire bicycling guide.

If you had taken every tour in the previous edition, you would have done twenty-seven rides and traveled about 760 miles. All those rides remain in this new edition—tested, reridden, rechecked, fine-tuned. The additions consist of seven new rides that contribute 350 fresh miles. Those, plus extensions and revisions of existing tours, make for about 1,160 miles in 30 excursions encompassing 37 rides. Most of the new rides are in what Governor Sherman Adams once called the "True North Country"—the land north of the Great Notches, with its surprisingly flat pastoral stretches of vistas of the Connecticut River Valley's upper reaches. This edition also has new rides in the Concord area and in Rockingham, Strafford, Merrimack, and Sullivan counties. Two revised rides visit the Christa McAuliffe Planetarium in Concord and Harrisville Village, a nineteenth-century industrial revolution community of splendid architecture. For the first time, the tours dip into Maine and Quebec, and so they now visit all of New Hampshire's neighbors, including Massachusetts and Vermont.

Above all, working on this book has given me a refreshed look at New Hampshire. Having to retrace those favorite routes with a new purpose has showed me once again just how beautiful New Hampshire is—the drama of the mountains, the sublime intervals of the far north, the coziness of the Monadnock Region, the serenity of the seacoast. We who live here are blessed. So come and enjoy these marvelous bicycle tours with us, and welcome to New Hampshire!

Adolphe Bernotas
Concord, October 1990

New Hampshire bicyclists help and advise their disabled colleagues.

Introduction

Bicycle tours can range from half-day trips around town to cross-country journeys. Touring is an activity in which nearly everyone can participate, from youngsters to grandparents. To us, bicycle touring provides an opportunity to be outdoors, where the air is clean and the scenery beautiful, where the terrain provides a bit of exercise and the countryside offers attractive spots for picnicking or an occasional shop for browsing. When we search for a tour, we look for something to make the day memorable.

For this guide we have put together 30 excursions that we hope do just that. They were chosen to bring out New Hampshire's varied beauty from the vantage point of the bicyclist on roads, disposed to biking and routes of reasonable length for the average cyclist. With very rare exceptions, cyclists must share the roads with motorized vehicles, and for this book we have chosen routes of least traffic to prevent the disappointment that can come when routes are selected at random from road maps.

Selecting a Tour

These loop tours, all of which end where they start, have been developed from our experience with The Biking Expedition, which has been operating trips for adults and teenagers since 1973, and from our personal knowledge of criss-crossing this splendid state and its neighbors along routes developed by the Granite State Wheelmen, a 1,500-member recreational bicycling club, one of the largest and most active such clubs in the country. The rides range in length from 10 miles to more than 100 miles, from easy to challenging. We've tried to remove the unpleasant surprises—but not the adventure!

The tours are organized roughly according to New Hampshire's tourism regions, starting with an easy pastoral ride in the state's southwestern corner and ending with grand trips north of the White Mountains into Canada. At the start of each tour, we summarize the distance, the ease or difficulty, and the terrain to allow you to decide whether it appeals to you, in the following format:

31.2 miles; easy to moderate cycling
Level to rolling terrain

If a ride catches your fancy, read on to discover specific information about lodging, points of interest, places to buy food, and road conditions. The tour's directions are set in **boldface** type, as are the cumulative mileage figures (the distance you have traveled to any particular point). Information about what you will encounter in terms of scenery, services, and road surfaces follows the **boldface** directions, in light type, like this:

5.9   Turn right on Grange Road and ride 11.2 miles to Groveton.

This section is as hilly as the ride will get. But you are rewarded with majestic views of mountains and meadows, pastures and streams. The road makes a sharp left at 8.0 miles and takes you into Lost Nation, where at 9.6 miles St. Timothy's Episcopal Chapel demands to be photographed. Here the road starts to ascend gradually, and then at about 12 miles climbs for 2 miles, with level respites, however. The recompense is a 3-mile downhill into Groveton.

Grange Road is a typical, narrow New Hampshire backcountry way, with smooth to rough surfaces, little or no shoulder, open in places with good visibility, shaded in others, and it has almost no traffic.

The evaluation of road conditions is based not on statistical traffic data but on our personal experience as bicyclists. Our criteria: apparent traffic volume, road width, shoulders, visibility or sight distance, and pavement condition. More heavily traveled roads are used only when absolutely necessary, and we point out these instances. However, unforeseen events may interfere and bring more traffic than we indicate. For instance, New Hampshire's splendid showing-off during the fall foliage season doesn't always arrive or leave on precise schedule, which may increase traffic along "leaf-peeper" roads. Or you may run into the state's Old Home Day tradition, a weekend when a particular community's backroads may be taxed by expatriates and inhabitants celebrating their hometowns.

Preparing for a Tour

As in all sports, in bicycle touring a few simple things can make the difference between a happy, fulfilling experience and a disappointing one. Before you start, you should know something about bicycle touring equipment, bicycle maintenance, your physical condition, and most important, bicycling safety.

Equipment. At a minimum for the average or beginning cyclist in New Hampshire, we recommend a wide-geared "rule of 30" 10-speed bike. That means a bike that weighs less than 30 pounds, with a rear-wheel cluster that has a sprocket with at least 30 teeth and a front chainring with a minimum of 30 teeth. A 12-, 15- and 18-speed bike with a "granny gear" is even better. While we have tried to include as many "flat" rides as possible, we cannot escape hills in New Hampshire. It lies at the northern end of the Appalachians, whose valleys can be flat but whose east-west passes bump against hills.

Make sure your bike has a rack to hold your panniers or a smaller pack to carry your things. A handlebar bag with a map case is a great convenience. Never wear a backpack while you are riding. Doing so is extremely unsafe because it raises your center of gravity, giving you about as much stability as a Mexican jumping bean. If you must carry a backpack, lash it down with bungee cords to your carrier, or use a fanny pack. Carry a bike lock. Carry food and at least one water bottle, and use it frequently. Remember this bicycling ditty, which applies to all sports: "Drink before thirsty, eat before hungry, rest before tired."

You will need a cyclocomputer to follow the distances of the routes in this book. Don't bother with an unreliable mechanical odometer. A suitable electronic cyclometer costs as little as $20. These devices now measure everything from cadence to elapsed time, average speed, highest speed, time in 12- or 24-hour clocks, miles per hour, kilometers per hour, and even pulse rate. Despite their sophistication, the devices must be set properly for your bicycle to extract accurate readings from them. Tire size, brand, pressure, even temperature (which affects tire pressure) can introduce variations. During an unscientific survey of six bicyclists on a recent ride, the Granite State Wheelmen found five slightly different readings within the first 8 miles, with each rider staking the mortgage money on the accuracy of his or her computer! So if the distances in this book don't always agree with yours to the last hair of the mile, please be gracious and give us and yourself some slack — and look carefully just before or after the bend for that turn!

Your bike should have a narrow, springless seat, turned-down handlebars, and toe clips. Despite their awkward appearance, these features have been refined for 100 years for comfort and cycling efficiency. For the shorter rides you can use off-road or mountain bikes if you change from knobby to slick tires; so-called hybrid bikes that combine off-road and road-bike features are adequate as well. If in doubt, check with your friendly local bike shop. Do not throw your money away on a poorly assembled, poor-quality bike from a department or discount store. Always patronize your bike professional, who will give you advice and guide you to books that will give you as much detail as you want on the proper care, feeding, and clothing of you and your machine. One such book, *Keep on Pedaling; The Complete Guide to Adult Bicycling* (Woodstock, VT: The Countryman Press, 1990), as its title suggests, demystifies biking with sensible advice on why, how, and where in the world to ride. Author Norman D. Ford is particularly persuasive about the physical, mental, and social benefits of bicycling at any age.

Bicycle Tools and Emergency Repairs. Even for a half-day tour, you should know how to make simple repairs, the most common of which is the flat tire. Carry at least one spare tube and patch kit, tire irons, and a pump. You should be able to confront a broken brake or derailleur cable by carrying a spare of each, plus a "third-hand tool" for the repair. Your toolkit should include needle-nose pliers capable of cutting cable, appropriate-sized wrenches to fit the nuts and bolts on your bike, flat and Phillips-head screwdrivers, and an adjustable wrench.

For longer trips, carry freewheel and chain tools, a spoke wrench and spare spokes, a crank tool, cone wrenches, spare brake blocks, a roll of electrical tape, spare nuts and bolts, lubricating oil, and a tube of grease. Your bike shop will outfit you with an appropriate touring bike toolkit.

If you break down in north-central New Hampshire (on tours 15, 24, 25, or 26), you can have the assistance of Cycle Fix, a bike shop on wheels. This is a bicycle road service, akin to car road services. Its phone number is listed at the end of each tour that lies in Cycle Fix's coverage area.

Other Emergencies. If you are faced with a problem your toolkit or biking partners can't solve and need immediate medical aid or the help of public safety authorities, call the following emergency police telephone numbers:

New Hampshire State Police
800-525-5555
800-852-3411
603-271-3636

Massachusetts State Police
800-525-5555
508-475-3800 (for Exeter-Massachusetts, Tour 21)
413-625-6311 (for Tri-Stater, Tour 1)

Maine State Police
(for New Hampshire-Maine, Tour 20)
800-525-5555
800-452-4664
207-439-1141

Vermont State Police
800-525-5555
802-748-3111 (for Waumbek Weekend, Tour 30)
802-254-3282 (for Tri-Stater, Tour 1)

Quebec Provencial Police (Sûreté)
(for Waumbek International Century, in Tour 30)
819-849-4813

Clothing. Clothing for bicycling is more than a fashion state-ment—it is for comfort. Eschew regular "sports" outfits! Wear biking shorts directly next to your skin—wearing underwear underneath biking shorts defeats their purpose of design. If you wear under-wear, you might as well spend your money on something else and ride in discomfort in your jogging shorts, gym shorts, or jeans. Wear bicycle jerseys, which are made of special natural and synthetic fibers designed to wick away moisture from your skin, keeping you cool in the heat and warm in the cold. Wear gloves, biking shoes, and sunglasses or goggles. Carry rain gear for the occasional outburst. Carry personal identification and coins for phone calls. Again, your bike shop is the place where you can get advice for your specific needs.

Physical Condition. People vary widely in cardiovascular effi-ciency, and the potential for overextending yourself exists in cycling as in any sport. Fortunately, cycling is an individual activity that you can undertake at your own pace. There's little excuse for overdoing it, and you have only yourself to blame for doing too much too soon. If you have been inactive physically or are more than 35 years old, or both, it's probably a good idea to have a physical checkup before you undertake the more strenuous tours. But a major advantage of cycling is that it is an activity in which you can participate throughout your life. Inexperienced cyclists tend to push gears that are too high, stressing their knees and lower back. Pedal at about 90 revolutions per minute. This may seem awkward at first, but the payoff is worth the effort. If you're a beginning cyclist, use this rule of thumb: Ride at least one gear lower than what at first feels comfortable, and spin more. With proper gearing and cycling techniques and consistent riding, your knees will last longer than they will under jogging, and your cardiovascular system will prosper.

Safety. Under New Hampshire law, bicycles are vehicles, sub-ject to the same rights, laws, and penalties as motor vehicles. Thus, the key rule for safe cycling is that if you wouldn't do it with a car, don't do it with the bike. That covers everything from riding on the wrong side of the road and on sidewalks, to taking left turns from right lanes, to disobeying traffic signs and signals. You wouldn't dream of driving your car on the left side of the road, or of taking a left turn from the right lane—taking the chance of being rammed in the side or getting a traffic ticket. You never would dream of driving your car on a sidewalk. Yet presumably intelligent adults violate these rules on bicycles. As with a car, don't follow another bike too closely, in case you have to make a sudden stop. Watch for parked car doors swinging open.

Your safety is not a function of the winsome hand signals you learned in fourth grade, or the redundancy of reflectors, or the goodwill of motorists. Your safety is a function of your position, attitude, and behavior on the road. Don't ride in the gutter. Ride with the traffic, sharing the road with other vehicles, and show the same common sense and courtesy when you bike as you do when you drive your car. Establish your position on the road and ride alertly, Teutonically. Ride predictably, and ride with self-assurance. These attitudes will show motorists that you are riding responsibly, and that you know what you are doing and will not do something unexpected.

Be aware of your surroundings. Don't use distracting headphones or radios. Use a rearview mirror. Watch out for sand patches that gather at intersections and turns, and parallel storm-sewer grates that can swallow your wheel and send you flying. Always cross railway tracks on a perpendicular. If the traffic won't allow it, dismount and walk — a technique that conquers any traffic problem! If you meet up with a dog, a sharp yell usually will turn the pooch aside, or you can use a dog-repellent chemical, spray ammonia, or one of the new electronic devices whose subsonic sounds stop canines dead in their tracks. You usually can outdistance a dog. Be visible — which means don't ride at night. Wear unnatural, non-earth tone colors.

Above all, don't even think of getting on a bicycle unless you are wearing a helmet. Broken bones, pulled muscles, and wrenched wrists will heal. A broken head will not.

Make sure your brakes work properly, and always use the real brake levers — not the so-called "safety levers" under the tops of the bars of cheaper bikes. Unless you have a pre-1970 French bicycle with Guidonnet levers, get rid of the "safety levers," which experienced cyclists with good reason have dubbed "suicide levers." Remove them so you're not tempted to use them.

The best source of information on bicycling, from maintenance to traffic flow theory, is *Effective Cycling* (Cambridge, MA: MIT Press, 1983) by John Forester, the foremost expert on biking, especially safety. That book will tell you in detail why you would be *non compos mentis* to ride on a sidewalk (where every driveway becomes an intersection), and the statistical and engineering reasons why you are far safer riding properly in city traffic than on certain bike paths (which usually are too narrow, are banked incorrectly, go nowhere, and must be shared with dogs, runners, children, other bicycles, and off-road machines). If you live in an area whose local bicycle club is affiliated with the League of American Wheelmen (LAW), join the group and take the "Effective Cycling" course based on Forester's principles. It covers everything from improving your riding technique to maintaining your bike to lobbying for bicycle-friendly legislation. The New Hampshire LAW affiliate is the Granite State Wheelmen (GSW), a marvelous resource. Indeed, New Hampshire's official tourism agency, the Office of Vacation Travel, routinely refers bicycling questions to the GSW. The GSW puts out an invaluable newsletter, *Pedal Talk,* that lists hundreds of rides in the state. Write to Granite State Wheelmen, Kathy Lacharite, 83 Londonderry Road, Windham NH 03087.

Monadnock Region

1

Tri-Stater

31.5 miles; easy to moderate cycling
Level to rolling terrain

While this is book about bicycle touring in New Hampshire, in the interest of safety and good touring, we have bent the ground rules somewhat for this loop through the fertile farmland of the Connecticut River Valley. Our Tri-Stater starts in southwestern New Hampshire, crosses into Northfield, Massachusetts, and winds back through Vernon and Brattleboro, Vermont. If you have completed one of the easy, half-day trips successfully, or if you wish to impress your friends with your superb physical and athletic ability by cycling in three states in one day, this is the trip for you. Actually, it is a great trip for anyone who can appreciate the majestic beauty of the Connecticut River and the serenity of country roads that twist and wind to open up new scenes around every bend.

Numerous motels offer lodging in the Brattleboro area. For a special treat, you might try the Chesterfield Inn and Restaurant (256-3211), on NH 9 in Chesterfield, New Hampshire, 1.6 miles east of the Vermont border. Recently renovated, this big old Colonial was until recently an antique carriage and sleigh museum. With beautiful views of the Vermont hills and the Connecticut River Valley to the west, it has lovely rooms, several of which contain fireplaces and whirlpools. In Northfield, Massachusetts, you can stay at Centennial House Bed and Breakfast (413-498-5921), located on MA 10/MA 63 across from the Northfield Fire Station, 0.9 mile south of Northfield Pizza House.

The tour begins at a wayside rest area on NH 119, about 1 mile south of the Hinsdale Raceway. Developed by Boy Scout Troop 307 in a shady pine grove next to the Connecticut River, the rest area offers sufficient room to park your car. It is easy to miss this spot, however. Look for a small rest area sign (a pine tree symbol with an arrow) just before the unpaved turn into the pine grove.

0.0 **From the rest area head east on NH 119 toward the center of Hinsdale for 2.7 miles to NH 63, on your right.**

On your way into Hinsdale you pass several other small wayside picnic areas with great views of the Connecticut River.

If you're approaching the starting point from the north, several

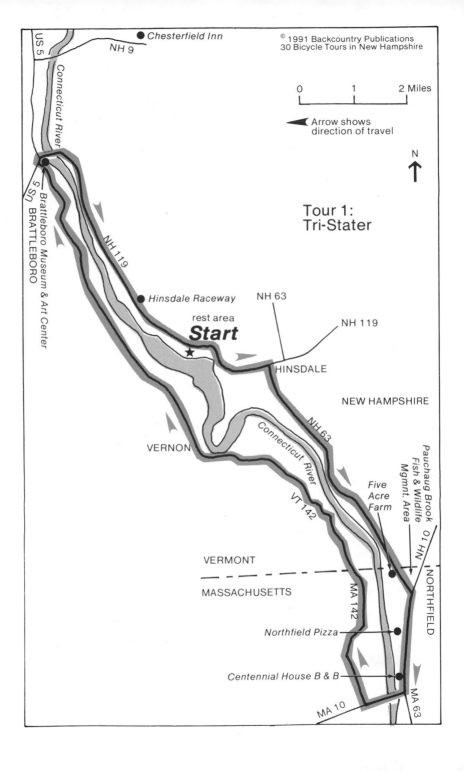

● Chesterfield Inn

US 5

NH 9

© 1991 Backcountry Publications
30 Bicycle Tours in New Hampshire

Connecticut River

0   1   2 Miles

◄ Arrow shows
   direction of travel

N

Tour 1:
Tri-Stater

US 5 BRATTLEBORO

Brattleboro Museum & Art Center

NH 119

● Hinsdale Raceway

NH 63

NH 119

rest area
Start

HINSDALE

NEW HAMPSHIRE

NH 63

VERNON

Connecticut River

Pauchaug Brook Fish & Wildlife Mgmnt. Area

NH 10

Five
Acre
Farm

VT 142

NORTHFIELD

VERMONT

MASSACHUSETTS

MA 142

Northfield Pizza

Centennial House B & B

MA 63

MA 10

Many productive, working farms dot the rolling countryside of the
Connecticut River Valley.

food stores line the stretch of NH 119 between the rest area and the raceway. Johnny's Drive-in, at the junction of NH 119 and NH 63 in Hinsdale, is open every day.

NH 119 in this area has a good surface but no shoulder except for a 0.4-mile section at the trip's beginning. The terrain is rolling with several short, moderately steep upgrades. Traffic is generally light to moderate.

2.7   Turn right onto NH 63 and ride south for 5.5 miles. You cross the state border into Northfield, Massachusetts, just before reaching MA 10.

A great road for cycling, NH 63 twists, dips, and turns as it hugs the eastern edge of the Connecticut River Valley. High enough to provide long views of corn fields and grazing cattle, yet without mind-blowing hills to challenge your legs and heart, it is a delight to ride. A small picnic area on the right, 3.2 miles from the NH 19/NH 63 junction, offers a nice spot to bask in the sun and enjoy the scenery. Five Acre Farm, located 0.5 mile before you reach MA 10, sells fresh vegetables during the summer. Pauchaug Brook Fish and Wildlife Management Area, operated by the Massachusetts Division of Fisheries and Wildlife, is at the junction of the two highways.

NH 63 is narrow with no shoulders, but it has a smooth surface. Visibility generally is good except at an occasional sharp turn or sudden dip. Traffic tends to be light.

8.2   At the intersection, turn right onto MA 10/MA 63 and ride 2.6 miles to where the two routes divide.

Northfield-Mount Hermon School, a coeducational boarding school, is set high above the Connecticut River, adjacent to MA 10/MA 63 on the northeast side of Northfield.

Several stores and restaurants await you in Northfield on MA 10/MA 63. Northfield Pizza House is 0.6 mile south of the MA 10/MA 63 junction. Northfield Country Store, 1.1 miles south of our turnoff, is open daily 8–8. The IGA directly across the street is also open all day, every day. Murray's Country Kitchen, adjacent to the IGA, is a small restaurant from which you can observe the gracious main street of Northfield, with its beautifully kept houses and manicured lawns.

MA 10/MA 63 is a wide two-lane road with a smooth surface. While it is a major route with some truck traffic, this short section that leads into town generally is safe to travel because the speed limit is low.

10.8   Turn right onto MA 10 and ride 1.8 miles to the junction with MA 142.

**12.6 At the intersection, turn right and head north on MA/VT 142 for
14.7 miles to VT 119 in Brattleboro.**

3.4 miles north of this intersection a general store offers food. At 6.5
miles, bear left at School House Grocery. Though small, it is well
stocked and has a deli (7:30–9 daily).

Much like NH 63 on the other side of the Connecticut River, this
route offers easy cycling through prosperous farm country, with
occasional views of the river. Two historical markers, one for Vernon's First Meeting House and the other for the tomb of Jemima
Tute (1723–1805), famed "fair captive," are located at 7.8 miles and
9.7 miles, respectively. The Brattleboro Museum and Art Center, at
the junction of VT 142 and US 5 in Brattleboro, is open Tuesday–Friday noon–4; Saturday and Sunday 1–4.

Brattleboro has many restaurants and food stores.

VT 142 is a smooth, narrow, two-lane road, with no shoulders
and light traffic. Visibility generally is good, except for a few areas
where curves and grades limit sight distance. For the most part the
terrain is quite flat, though there are a few rolling hills. Be alert for
several railroad crossings, especially near Brattleboro.

**27.3 At the intersection, turn right toward New Hampshire, head down
a short hill (beware of the railroad tracks at the bottom!), and
cross the Connecticut River.**

**As you cross, the road becomes NH 119. Continue for 4.2
miles to your car.**

NH 119 is a wide road with good visibility. Initially the shoulder is
poor, but later it widens to a smooth paved surface as you near
Hinsdale Raceway. Traffic is generally light to moderate, except
during racing times at the harness track, when it can be heavy.
There is one short, steep hill to climb soon after you cross the bridge
over the Connecticut.

**31.5 You made it! You are back at the rest area where you began your
trip.**

Bicycle Repair Services
The Bicycle Barn, 56 Main Street, Northfield MA (9–5 Mon.–Sat.) (413-498-2996)
Brattleboro Bicycle Shop, 178 Main Street, Brattleboro VT (10–6 Mon.–Fri.; 10–5
    Sat.) (802-254-8644)
Specialized Sports, Putney Road, Brattleboro VT (10–6 Mon.–Fri.; 10–4 Sat.)
    (802-257-1071)

2

Swanzey Covered Bridges

18.3 miles; easy cycling
Level to rolling terrain

Covered bridges are as characteristic of New Hampshire as maple syrup, baked beans, and church suppers. They assure us of the comfort of permanence and continuity with the past and provide an escape from the plastic and glitter of twentieth-century life. Swanzey, in the southwestern corner of the state, is the proud possessor of four such spans, all conveniently connected by gently rolling country roads. This tour extends into Winchester for yet a fifth bridge. On this tour, an excellent beginning trip for adults and children, you experience a kinship with early farmers and settlers who, like you, traveled these byways and crossed these bridges with no help from the internal combustion engine.

When you reach these relics, examine how they are put together. Covered bridges originally were built to carry loaded haywagons over rivers, and since they were designed and constructed by local farmers, each has its own character. The roof and siding that cover a bridge (which had to be high enough to accommodate the loaded wagons) were meant primarily to safeguard the truss work, not passersby, from the elements.

Overnight accommodations can be found in Keene (3 miles to the north). See our Surry Mountain–Gilsum tour (Tour 3) for suggestions.

The starting point for this tour is the junction of NH 32 and Sawyers Crossing Road, in the center of Swanzey. Monadnock Regional High School and Swanzey Town Hall, both adjacent to this intersection, have parking lots where you can leave your car.

0.0   From the high school or town hall in Swanzey, head south on NH 32 for 1.5 miles to Carlton Road, on your left.

NH 32 is a two-lane road with no shoulder, a smooth surface, good visibility, and low traffic. The terrain is mostly level.

1.5   At Carlton Road, turn left and travel 1.1 miles, passing through your first covered bridge, to the junction with Webber Hill Road.

The Carlton covered bridge, over South Brook, is thought to be one of the oldest in the area. Rebuilt in 1990, it was constructed in the

Queenpost truss style, a design used on the earliest bridges that farmers built employing the same methods they used for their churches and barns. Although once quite common, few bridges constructed in this style stand today.

Carlton Road is quite level, except for one moderate upgrade just beyond the bridge. It is narrow and has no shoulder, little traffic, and a good surface for cycling.

2.6 **At the T-junction turn right on Webber Hill Road, head downhill past the East Swanzey Post Office, and then bear right as you merge with another unmarked road by the Swanzey Fire Department East Company. A biker's delight with a smooth, level surface, this road brings you back to NH 32 in 1.3 miles.**

The backroads in this area are much alike—narrow with no shoulder, with reasonably smooth surfaces, occasional frost heaves, and slightly rolling terrain.

3.9 **At the intersection, bear right on NH 32, riding north for 0.1 mile to Swanzey Lake Road (unmarked) on the left.**

4.0 **Turn left onto Swanzey Lake Road and ride for 3.9 miles to a T-junction with an unmarked road.**

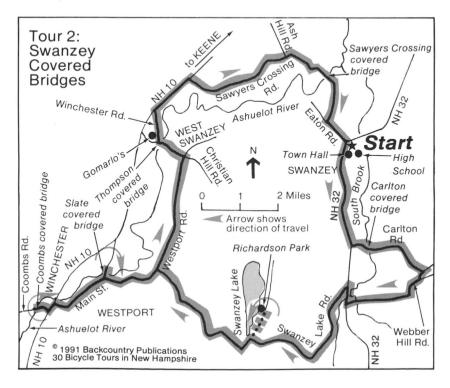

Tour 2: Swanzey Covered Bridges

© 1991 Backcountry Publications
30 Bicycle Tours in New Hampshire

For swimming, bear right off Swanzey Lake Road onto the road that rings Swanzey Lake. In about 0.3 mile you'll come to Richardson Park, which offers swimming and picnicking for a small admission charge.

Swanzey Lake Road is similar to the other backcountry roads you travel on this tour. It has several twists and turns, but if you stay on the surfaced road, you should not get lost.

7.9   **At the T-junction turn left onto the (unmarked) Westport Road, and ride 0.8 mile to a stop sign, at Main Street (unmarked).**

8.7   **Turn left at the stop sign at Main Street (unmarked) and ride 0.7 mile to the junction of NH 10 in Westport, a village on the Swanzey-Winchester town line.**

9.4   **At the T-junction turn left onto NH 10 South and pedal 0.3 mile to Coombs Road (unmarked), preceded by a black-on-yellow right-turn sign.**

By 9.6 miles, you're in Winchester. On your left you pass the friendly folks at Affordable Bicycle Repair, worth a stop for a chat.

NH 10 is a major road with moderate traffic, but it is wide and well-surfaced, with excellent visibility and shoulders.

9.7   **Turn right at Coombs Road (unmarked) at a white house with a pine tree in the yard and ride 0.3 mile to the Coombs covered bridge.**

10.0   **Cross the Coombs bridge, turn around, and retrace 0.3 mile to NH 10.**

The 118-foot Coombs bridge, built in 1837, was rebuilt in 1972 on stone abutments without mortar. Like the rest of the covered bridges on this tour, it spans the Ashuelot River *(pronounced Ash-WEE-lut)* and is of Town lattice truss construction, a design developed in the 1830s by Ithiel Town, a renowned engineer of his time.

(If your get-up-and-go hasn't got up and went, an extra 20-or-so miles rewards you with one of New Hampshire's grandest covered bridges: at the west end of the Coombs bridge, bear south on Old Westport Road to Winchester, then west on NH 119 to the 160-foot, double-span Ashuelot, considered "pure American Gothic architecture adopted to bridge building.")

10.3   **Turn left onto NH 10 North and ride 0.3 mile back to Westport Road.**

10.6   **At Westport Road and signs for Swanzey Lake and Richmond, turn right and ride 0.7 mile to a fork.**

11.3   As you near the fork, Westport Road bears right, while Main Street (unmarked) veers left across the Slate covered bridge, which is in your view. Ride 0.1 mile to the bridge.

11.4   Cross the Slate bridge, then return 0.1 mile to the stop sign back at Westport Road.

The original 142-foot Slate bridge, built in 1800 and rebuilt in 1862, includes iron turnbuckle rods in its design.

11.5   At the stop sign make a hairpin left turn back onto Westport Road and ride for 1.4 miles to a three-way stop, at the intersection of Christian Hill Road.

13.9   At the three-way stop, turn left onto Christian Hill Road and ride 0.3 miles to the Thompson covered bridge.

The double-span, 155-foot bridge was built in 1832 by Zodoc Taft at a cost of $532.27. The bridge had two sidewalks, only one of which remains.

14.2   Cross the Thompson bridge and take the immediate right onto Winchester Road (unmarked), and ride 0.4 mile to the junction of NH 10.

Photo by Eric Sanford/NH Office of Vacation Travel

The Thompson Bridge still has one of its two sidewalks.

At the west end of the bridge, Gomarlo's Food and Circus is a nice stop for refreshments.

14.6 At the junction, turn right onto NH 10 North and ride 0.6 mile to Sawyers Crossing Road.

Nick's Restaurant is on NH 10 South, a few hundred yards to the left of this junction.

NH 10 is a major road with moderate traffic, but for the half-mile-plus that you're on it, its visibility, surface, and shoulders are excellent.

15.2 Turn right onto Sawyers Crossing Road and ride 1.4 miles to the junction where Ash Hill Road comes in from the left.

16.6 Bearing right at this junction stay on Sawyers Crossing Road and ride 0.7 mile to the Sawyers Crossing covered bridge.

At 159 feet, Sawyers Crossing is the longest covered bridge on your tour. Built in the 1830s at a cost of $1,735.64, it was rebuilt in 1859.

17.3 Traverse Sawyers Crossing bridge and ride 0.6 mile to a stop sign at Eaton Road.

17.9 Turn left onto Eaton Road and ride 0.4 mile to the junction of NH 32 in the center of Swanzey.

18.3 You're back where you started, five covered-bridge crossings to your credit!

Bicycle Repair Services

Affordable Bike Repair, NH 10, Winchester-Swanzey town line (10–6 Mon.–Fri.) (357-7510, 357-8353)

Andy's Cycle, 165 Winchester Street, Keene (9–6 Mon.–Fri.; 9–5 Sat.; 10–4 Sun., March–Aug.) (352-3410)

Joe Jones Ski and Sport Shop, 222 West Street, Keene (10–9 Mon.–Sat.; 11–6 Sun.) (352-5266)

Norm's Ski and Bike Shop, Martel Court (NH 9/NH 12/NH 101), Keene (10–6 Mon., Tues., Thur., Sat.; 10–9 Fri.; closed Wed. and Sun.) (352-1404)

Summers Backcountry Sports, 16 Ashuelot Street, Keene (9–7 Mon.–Wed.; 9–9 Thur.–Fri.; 9–7 Sat.; 11–4 Sun.) (357-5107)

3
Surry Mountain-Gilsum

22.5 miles; moderate to challenging cycling
Rolling to hilly terrain, one major hill

Because it offers variety, our trip around Surry Mountain, just north of Keene, can be approached in several ways. It is ideal for cyclists who seek the solitude of an early-morning ride along the Ashuelot River (pronounced *Ash-WEE-lut*), the challenge of a steep hill near Gilsum, and the exhilaration of a long descent into Keene. Those who wish a full day's outing have their choice of many activities to break up the cycling: a stop in Keene, an active college town, is the perfect counterpoint to a trip through the countryside; the Surry Mountain Recreation Area, whose dam and reservoir were built as a flood-control project, offers outdoor activities from swimming to camping; and Gilsum, a site of about 60 inactive mines that a century ago produced beryl, rose quartz, and even gold, is an enticing detour.

Keene, the Elm City, was chartered in 1753 as Upper Ashuelot and was incorporated in 1873. It is the Cheshire County seat and the Monadnock Region's largest community. Whether its elegant central thoroughfare is indeed the country's widest main street remains a topic of discourse.

Keene has several motels and inns including: Valley Green Motel, 379 West Street (352-7350), Winding Brook Lodge, Park Avenue (352-3111), and the Ramada Inn at the junction of NH 10 and NH 101 (357-3038). For more homelike accommodations, try the Carriage Barn Guest House (357-3812) on Main Street, across from the campus of Keene State College. Pack a lunch in Keene because there are no food stops elsewhere on this route.

The trip begins at Surry Mountain Recreation Area on NH 12A, 5.5 miles north of Central Square in Keene. On your way from Keene, do not follow Dam Road, which leads to the dam and office building. Continue 1.1 miles past this road to the entrance of the day-use area, on the right, where a large parking lot, changing house, beach, picnic tables, and well-maintained grounds are located. The parking lot can be used from May through September; it is flooded at other times.

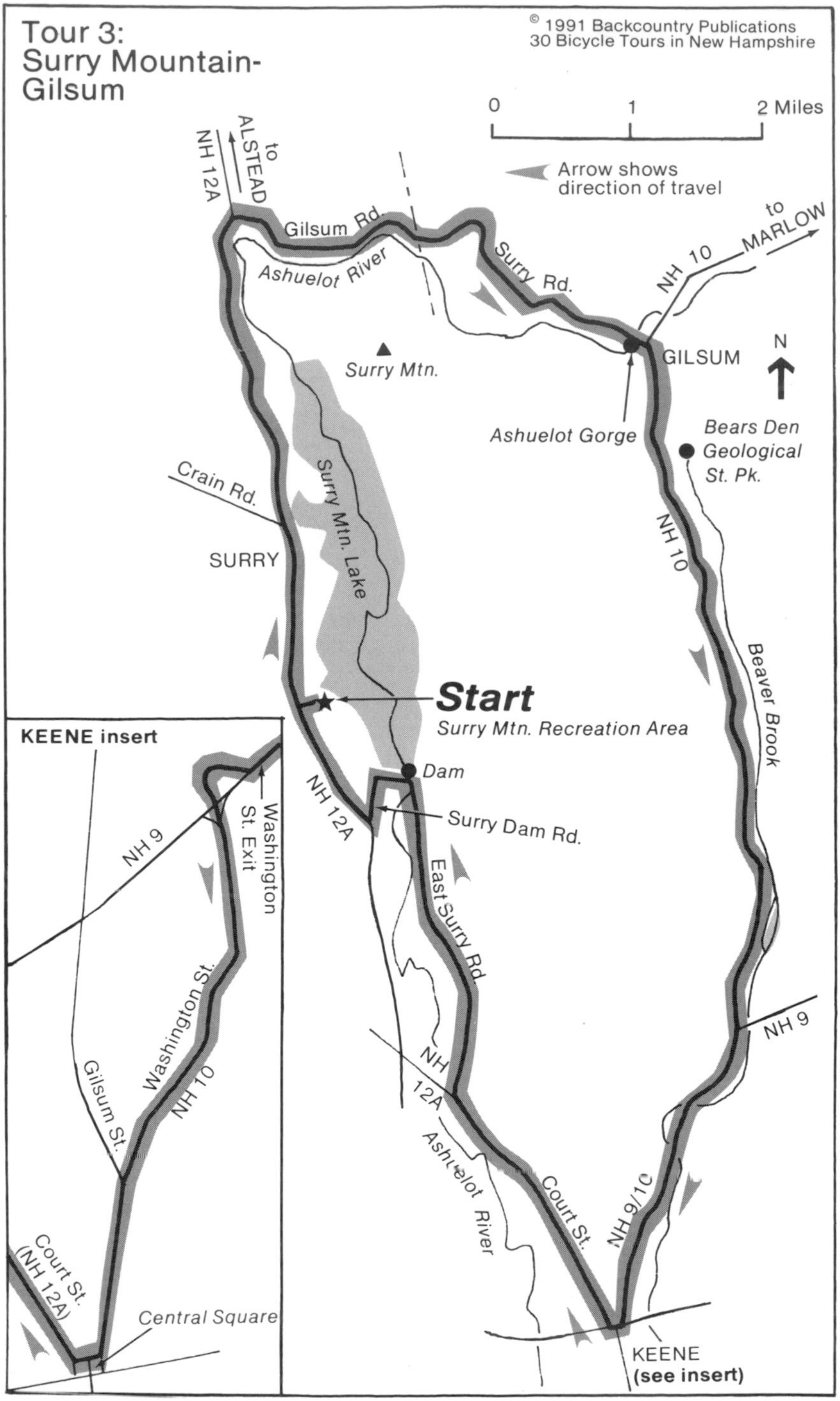

Tour 3:
Surry Mountain-
Gilsum

© 1991 Backcountry Publications
30 Bicycle Tours in New Hampshire

0   1   2 Miles

◄ Arrow shows
direction of travel

to ALSTEAD

NH 12A

Gilsum Rd.

Ashuelot River

Surry Rd.

NH 10

to MARLOW

▲ Surry Mtn.

GILSUM

N

Ashuelot Gorge

Bears Den
Geological
St. Pk.

Crain Rd.

SURRY

Surry Mtn. Lake

NH 10

Beaver Brook

Start

Surry Mtn. Recreation Area

KEENE insert

Dam

Surry Dam Rd.

NH 9

NH 12A

Washington St. Exit

East Surry Rd

NH 9

Washington St.

Gilsum St.

NH 10

NH 12A

Ashuelot River

Court St.

NH 9/10

Court St. (NH 12A)

Central Square

KEENE
(see insert)

0.0 **From the parking lot, return to NH 12A and turn right, heading north for 3.7 miles to Gilsum Road, on your right.**

Surry Mountain Recreation Area offers swimming, boating, hiking, picnicking, fishing, and camping. The village of Surry is 1.1 miles north of the recreation area entrance, off NH 12A on Crain Road.

NH 12A has a smooth surface and good visibility, but only a narrow shoulder. The terrain is flat to rolling. Traffic tends to be light but picks up during commuting hours.

3.7 **Turn right onto Gilsum Road and proceed for 4.3 miles to NH 10.**

Here you wind alongside the Ashuelot River through a small valley where the vegetation varies from thick forest to open meadow. Ashuelot Gorge, at the junction of Gilsum Road and NH 10, is worth a look from the stone arch bridge that spans it. If you turn left on NH 10 and ride toward Gilsum, you can swim on your left in the Ashuelot. If you wish to explore old mines or dig for semi-precious stones, stop at the Gilsum Village Store, established 1881 (open all day every day), or write to the Gilsum Library (Box 57, Gilsum NH 03448) for a copy of an area map ($.25). If your timing is right, you can attend Gilsum's annual Rock Swap, held during the last week of June, when hundreds of rockhounds trade, dig, and buy semi-precious stones.

The two-lane Gilsum Road, which at the Gilsum town line becomes Surry Road, is narrow, with no shoulder and a moderately bumpy surface. Because of its many twists and turns, visibility is limited; however, traffic is very light. The terrain is moderately hilly with a gradual rise as you proceed upstream along the Ashuelot. A steep 0.3-mile downgrade with a sharp turn awaits you 3 miles after turning on Gilsum Road. Caution is advised.

8.0 **Turn right onto NH 10 South and immediately begin a steep 0.8-mile climb, the trip's most difficult, and continue for a total of 5.2 miles to the junction of NH 10 and NH 9.**

NH 10, a major north-south highway, has a smooth surface, adequate width, generally good visibility, and an intermittent shoulder that turns to a nicely paved, full breakdown lane as you approach Keene.

With the exception of the steep hill immediately south of Gilsum Road, the terrain is either level or slopes down toward Keene. Except for peak periods on weekends, traffic usually is acceptable.

13.2 **At the junction of NH 10 and NH 9, where the two roads become one, turn right and ride 0.9 mile to the Washington Street Exit.**

NH 9/NH 10 is a four-lane highway with good visibility but little shoulder, ascending about 0.5 mile, then narrowing to two lanes but offering a wide paved breakdown lane.

14.1 **Bearing right, take the Washington Street Exit and ride 0.3 mile to a stop sign, cross NH 9/NH 10, and continue on Washington Street another 1.2 miles, where Gilsum Street merges with Washington.**
As you descend the exit ramp, avoid storm sewers with parallel grates that could grab your wheel and flip you!

15.6 **Bear left on Washington as Gilsum merges from the right and ride 0.5 mile to Central Square.**

16.1 **In downtown Keene, proceed about one-quarter of the way around Central Square, turn sharply right onto Court Street (also NH 12A) near The Stage restaurant, and continue 2.1 miles to East Surry Road (note the sign for Bretwood Golf Course).**

There's no better way to see New Hampshire than from a bicycle.

Photo by Jon-Pierre Lasseigne

Many fine Colonial and Victorian homes line the streets around Central Square. Keene State College, Thorne Art Gallery, and Wyman Tavern are but a few of the many attractions in this community.

Brando's Deli on Washington Street across from the junior high school makes great sandwiches (6–6 Mon.–Fri., 7–5 Sat.).

Keene has many fine restaurants: two of them are "176 Main" (11:30–11 Mon.–Thurs., 11:30–12 Fri.–Sat., and 11:30–10 Sun.); and Henry David's, 81 Main Street (11:30–11:30 daily, 352-0608).

Court Street has moderate-to-heavy traffic. For 0.8 mile, its wide shoulder also is used for parking, so be alert for opening car doors in your path. The road is reasonably flat.

18.2   **At East Surry Road, bear right and ride for 2.8 miles to Surry Dam Road.**

East Surry Road is smooth, with no shoulder and low traffic. Don't follow the road as it makes a sharp left turn and goes over a small bridge beyond the golf course. Stay on the paved road.

21.0   **At Surry Dam Road, turn left and ride for 0.4 mile to NH 12A.**

Surry Dam Road also is smooth, with no shoulder and little traffic.

21.4   **At the junction of NH 12A, make a hairpin right turn and cycle 1.1 miles back to the Surry Mountain Recreation Area.**

22.5   **You are at the entrance to the day-use area and the end of your trip.**

Bicycle Repair Services

Andy's Cycle, 165 Winchester Street, Keene (9–6 Mon.–Fri.; 9–5 Sat.; 10–4 Sun., March–Aug.) (352-3410)

Joe Jones Ski and Sport Shop, 222 West Street, Keene (10–9 Mon.–Sat.; 11–6 Sun.) (352-5266)

Norm's Ski and Bike Shop, Martel Court (NH 9/NH 12/NH 101), Keene (10–6 Mon., Tues., Thur., Sat.; 10–9 Fri.; closed Wed. and Sun.) (352-1404)

Summers Backcountry Sports, 16 Ashuelot Street, Keene (9–7 Mon.–Wed.; 9–9 Thur.–Fri.; 9–7 Sat.; 11–4 Sun.) (357-5107)

4
Alstead-Marlow

27.5 miles; challenging cycling
Level to hilly terrain

Alstead, Marlow, South Acworth, and Langdon: vintage New Hampshire at its best! Here there are no resorts or suburban developments — only tree-shaded lanes along mountain brooks that tumble and roll on their way to the Connecticut River, and individualists whose spirit and fortitude are infectious. Here, in New Hampshire's major maple-syrup-producing region, life is neither hurried nor complicated. While some bicycle tours should be approached as experiences in solitude, this is not one of them; the residents of these towns are more than willing to share themselves and their experiences.

The area's history is peopled with singular characters. Alstead (rhymes with *gal's head*) was named in 1763 not after an English lord or county but after the German encyclopedist, theologian, and philosopher Johann Heinrich Alstead, more than a century after his death. The community once was known as Paper Village, for it was on the Cold River in Alstead in 1793, and not in the state's northern woods, where New Hampshire's first paper mill was established. In the last century, Marlow — named after the sixteenth-century playwright and author Christopher Marlowe — gave the world Calista Huntley, one of America's first concert pianists, as well as "Rosina Delight" Richardson, who by age 19 weighed 515 pounds and joined General Tom Thumb and Commodore Nutt (of Manchester, New Hampshire) in P. T. Barnum's circus as "Fat Rosie." In its earlier days, South Acworth achieved fame for the cultivation of flax used for weaving linen; its Congregational Church, built in 1821, is considered to be among New England's most architecturally beautiful structures.

Another architectural landmark, Langdon's 1802 rectangular town hall, can be enjoyed with a slight northerly detour of about a mile from the starting point of this ride on NH 12A. Langdon was incorporated in 1787, its S-shaped area carved out of Charlestown and Walpole and christened after statesman John Langdon, New Hampshire's second governor, Revolutionary soldier, shipbuilder, and president pro-tem of the Senate in the first Congress of the United States. Known as the "Quiet

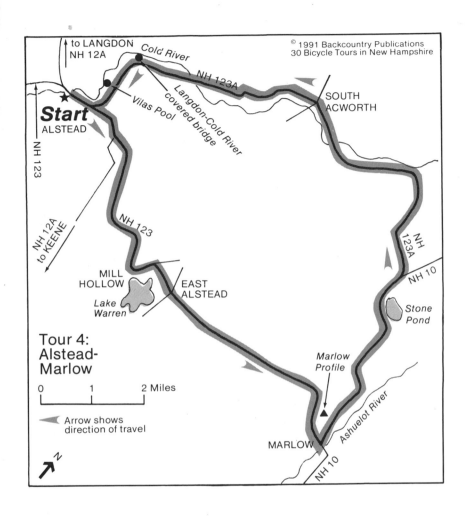

Community," this village of 580 people has changed little over the decades; its population peaked at 666 in 1830.

Because you are touring rugged land that rises upward and eastward from the Connecticut River Valley, this tour is not particularly easy. In fact, about a quarter of the route, 6.5 miles, involves a climb—some of it steep. But the rest is either flat or downhill! It's not a bad ratio, especially since you do the climbing early in the trip. And your efforts are rewarded by outstanding scenery and about 16 miles of effortless biking. If you're a racer or triathloner, this is the perfect training ride – climbs, flats, and downhill plunges!

The tour begins in the village of Alstead, on NH 12A/NH 123, approximately 25 miles north of Keene. Main Street, the numbered highway, offers ample opportunity for on-street parking.

For accommodations, we suggest Darby Brook Farm (835-6624) on Hill Road in Alstead. Operated by Howard Weeks, this inn is located in a quiet country setting and is open May through October. Or try the Cupola House in East Alstead, on NH 123 (835-6459).

0.0   **Begin by traveling east on Main Street (NH 12A/NH 123), past the stores and school, for 0.7 mile to the junction with NH 123A.**

The Village Store (7–9 Mon.–Sat.; 8–9 Sun.), on Alstead's Main Street, is the only grocery where you can buy food until you reach the Mill Hollow Store, at 4.6 miles. Check the village bulletin board next to the entrance for local events of interest.

NH 12A/ NH 123 is smooth and wide, with very little shoulder and light-to-moderate traffic.

0.7   **At the junction, take the right fork and continue on NH 12A/NH 123 toward Keene for another 0.7 mile, where the road forks again.**

1.4   **At the fork, stay left on NH 123 where NH 12A heads south to Keene. Continue through Mill Hollow and East Alstead for 9 miles to NH 10 in Marlow.**

This stretch offers numerous views of farmland set against mountains. Mill Hollow, a late-eighteenth-century community of small, individually operated mills, still has a standing grist mill. East Alstead is a hilltop town with well-kept homes and a splendid view of Lake Warren to the southwest. The Cupola House bed and breakfast and the Mill Hollow Store are on your right at 4.6 miles by the lake, a delicious swimming spot.

Four miles beyond East Alstead you pass beneath the Marlow Profile, a rocky cliff that bears a close resemblance to New Hampshire's symbolic Old Man of the Mountain.

Breshear's Farm Stand is 1.2 miles from Alstead, on the right side of NH 123.

After NH 12A splits off toward Keene, NH 123 narrows and the shoulder disappears. However, the visibility is good and there is little traffic. You climb about 6.5 miles to Marlow. For the most part the slope is gradual with occasional steep pitches, sometimes relieved by a level stretch or downgrade.

10.4   **At the junction of NH 123 and NH 10 in Marlow, turn left on NH 10
and ride north for 4.4 miles to NH 123A, on your left.**

In Marlow, the grounds around a lily pond offer a pleasant rest stop.
About 0.1 mile to the right on NH 10, PC Connection, a computer
mail-order house, has restored for corporate use a former Victorian
mansion of solid elegance. The Ashuelot (pronounced *Ash-WEE-lut*)
River and Stone Pond along your route offer swimming and picnicking.

The Marlow Village Store & Deli (8–7 daily) is at the junction of
NH 123 and NH 10.

NH 10 is smooth, with an intermittent shoulder and moderate
traffic, but the visibility is good and the terrain quite flat.

Photo by Susan Heavey

The Cold River's undisturbed banks offer a refreshing rest on the Alstead-
Marlow tour.

14.8 **At the junction, turn left and follow NH 123A west for 10.2 miles downhill through South Acworth to NH 12A/NH 123, back into Alstead.**

Cold River, a shallow, rocky stream paralleling the road, offers frequent opportunities for a refreshing wade, particularly by a bridge to your left at 19.6 miles.

In South Acworth the Village Store, founded in 1865, is open Monday through Saturday 7–7, Sunday 8–5. 3.8 miles beyond South Acworth you pass on your extreme right the Langdon–Cold River covered bridge, a 78-foot span built in 1869 by Albert Granger.

Just before you reach NH 12A/NH 123 again, you coast past Vilas Pool (11–7), a popular swimming and picnic area that offers swan boat rides in the summer.

The first 2.1 miles on NH 123A descend steeply alongside a tree-shaded brook. On a sunny day the lacy shadows can hide the bumps and cracks in the road. The road turns sharply left at the bottom of this steep stretch. The remaining miles to Alstead slope less steeply downward along the narrow and winding shoulderless road.

25.0 **At the junction turn right onto NH 12A/NH 123 to retrace the last 0.7 mile to Alstead.**

25.7 **You are back where you started.**

Bicycle Repair Services
There are no bike shops on this tour. The nearest are:
Andy's Cycle, 165 Winchester Street, Keene (9–6 Mon.–Fri.; 9–5 Sat.; 10–4 Sun., March–Aug.) (352-3410)
Joe Jones Ski and Sport Shop, 222 West Street, Keene (10–9 Mon.–Sat.; 11–6 Sun.) (352-5266)
Norm's Ski and Bike Shop, Martel Court (NH 9/NH 12/NH 101), Keene (10–6 Mon., Tues., Thur., Sat.; 10–9 Fri.; closed Wed. and Sun.) (352-1404)
Ped'ling Fool, 77 West Main Street, Hillsboro (10–1 Mon., Tues., Thurs., Fri.; 9–5 Sat.) (464-5286)
Summers Backcountry Sports, 16 Ashuelot Street, Keene (9–7 Mon.–Wed.; 9–9 Thur.–Fri.; 9–7 Sat.; 11–4 Sun.) (357-5107)
West Hill Shop, I-91 Exit 4, Putney VT (10–6 daily) (802-367-5718)

5
Jaffrey-Fitzwilliam

20.6 miles; moderate cycling
Rolling terrain, some short, steep hills

Mount Monadnock, rising nearly 2,000 feet above surrounding hills to a peak of 3,165 feet, dominates southwestern New Hampshire's landscape. Tucked in its shadow are the towns of Jaffrey, Rindge and Fitzwilliam, whose rolling terrain and secondary roads make for delightful bicycling. Since this tour is relatively short and only moderately demanding, it can be combined easily with stops at historic sites and antique shops or a side trip up Mount Monadnock, which has surpassed Japan's Fuji as the world's most-climbed mountain.

Three elegant inns that provide food and lodging are the Fitzwilliam Inn (585-9000) in Fitzwilliam, the Woodbound Inn (532-8341) in Rindge, and the Monadnock Inn (532-7001) in Jaffrey Center. The tour route goes by each.

Begin your tour in Jaffrey at the junction of US 202, NH 137, and NH 124. Ample parking is available along the main street and in the municipal parking lot.

0.0 **From Jaffrey, head west on NH 124 for 4.5 miles through Jaffrey Center to Fitzwilliam Road, on your left. A red farmhouse on your right marks this turn.**

The Jaffrey Civic Center, on the right side of NH 124 just west of the US 202/NH 137 junction, is the place to pick up information about the area's fascinating history and people. They include Willa Cather, the Pulitzer-prize-winning writer buried in Jaffrey Center; Amos Fortune, a black slave who bought his freedom in Massachusetts at the age of 59 and then moved to Jaffrey in 1781, where he established a tannery and lived as a highly respected citizen until his death in 1801; and Hannah Davis, a spinster left destitute at the age of 34 who supported herself by making wooden hat boxes, which since have become collector's items.

The Civic Center is open Monday through Saturday 1:30–5 (532-6527 or 532-8811). In Jaffrey Center, which you pass through in 1.6 miles, several historic homes and buildings—including the Old Meeting House, First Church, Amos Fortune's grave, and The

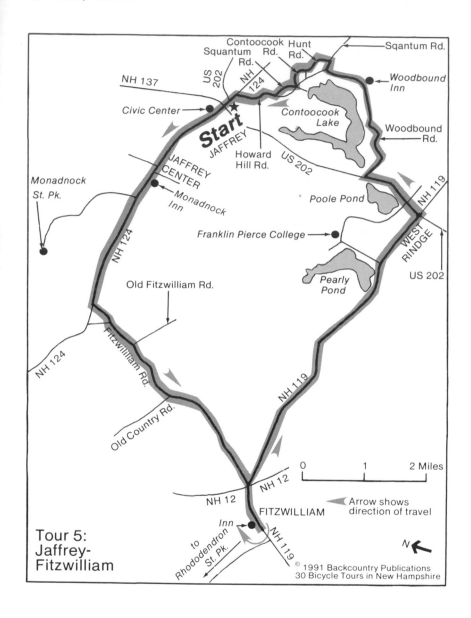

Sqantum Rd.

Contoocook Hunt
Squantum   Rd.   Rd.
Rd.

NH 137

US 202

NH 124

Civic Center

Woodbound
Inn

Contoocook
Lake

Start

JAFFREY

Woodbound
Rd.

Howard
Hill Rd.

US 202

JAFFREY
CENTER

Monadnock
St. Pk.

Monadnock
Inn

Poole Pond

NH 124

Franklin Pierce College

NH 119

WEST
RINDGE

US 202

Old Fitzwilliam Rd.

Pearly
Pond

Fitzwilliam Rd.

NH 124

Old Country Rd.

NH 119

0   1   2 Miles

NH 12

NH 12

FITZWILLIAM

Arrow shows
direction of travel

Tour 5:
Jaffrey-
Fitzwilliam

Inn

to
Rhododendron
St. Pk.

NH 119

N

© 1991 Backcountry Publications
30 Bicycle Tours in New Hampshire

Little Red Schoolhouse—beckon you to stop and admire.

The area's natural history is explained at Monadnock State Park. The turn is 0.5 mile beyond Jaffrey Center. The road leads 2 miles into the park to Monadnock Ecocenter, operated by the Society for the Protection of New Hampshire Forests at the trailhead of the White Dot Trail, which leads up the famous mountain.

The fifteen-room Monadnock Inn, an 1830 tavern, is 0.2 mile on the left beyond Jaffrey Center (lunch 11:30–2 Mon.–Fri.; dinner 5:30–9 Mon.–Sat., 5–8 Sun.; brunch 10–2 Sun.).

Stores and restaurants abound in Jaffrey, the last place to buy food until you reach Fitzwilliam.

From Jaffrey to Jaffrey Center, NH 124 is smooth, with a wide paved shoulder. Visibility is good, the terrain gentle, and the traffic moderate. As you leave Jaffrey Center, the road narrows and the shoulder disappears.

4.5 **At Fitzwilliam Road, turn left and follow this road 4.2 miles to its junction with NH 12 in Fitzwilliam. Note that Old Fitzwilliam Road joins Fitzwilliam Road from the left after 0.9 mile. Do not go left on Old Fitzwilliam Road. Follow Fitzwilliam Road for 0.2 mile beyond this junction where the road forks again. Old Country Road veers to the right; you stay left on Fitzwilliam Road.**

Fitzwilliam Road is a narrow backcountry road with a smooth surface, no shoulder, good visibility, and very little traffic.

8.7 **At this intersection, cross NH 12 and immediately join NH 119 in Fitzwilliam. Merge right on NH 119 and follow NH 119 a short distance to the village green, circle, then retrace your route to the junction of NH 12 and NH 119.**

In Fitzwilliam several antique shops are worth visiting. The Fitzwilliam Inn on the Common has been offering passersby lodging, food, and good cheer since 1796. The Inn serves lunch noon–2 and dinner 6–9:30 daily. The meeting house and Blake House, two more historical buildings on the green, also are worth noting. For a side trip, 2.6 miles southwest of the Fitzwilliam green takes you to Rhododendron State Park. Encompassing 16 acres of wild rhododendrons, it's one of the largest tracts of this species north of the Allegheny Mountains. The bumpy, hilly road is well worth a visit in mid-July, when the blossoms are at their peak.

NH 12 and NH 119 through Fitzwilliam are narrow, with moderately heavy but slow-moving traffic.

9.4 **Cross NH 12 and head straight toward West Rindge along NH 119 for 5.5 miles to the junction with US 202.**

Franklin Pierce College, on your left 4 miles east of Fitzwilliam, is a four-year, liberal arts school founded in 1962. It has more than 700 students.

NH 119 is recently resurfaced but has no shoulder. It takes you over rolling terrain with moderately heavy traffic and excellent visibility.

14.9 **At West Rindge, turn left onto US 202 and follow it north 1.2 miles past Poole Pond (on your left) to an unmarked road on your right just beyond a sign for Woodmere Campground and Woodbound Inn.**

Old Forge Restaurant (noon–3, 5–9 Tues.–Sat.; noon–8 Sun.) is located on US 202, 0.3 mile from its junction with NH 119, and features country cooking.

US 202 is wider than NH 119 and has an eight-foot paved shoulder. While US 202 is a major route, its wide shoulder and excellent visibility make it appealing for cycling.

16.1 **Beyond the sign for the campground, turn right onto Woodbound Road (unmarked) and follow it for 0.3 mile.**

Once you leave US 202, the roads back to Jaffrey are typical rural New Hampshire lanes. Winding over rolling terrain, they have bumpy surfaces, no shoulders, and fair visibility with little traffic.

Photo by Amy Wallace

The Fitzwilliam Inn, one of three typical New Hampshire inns on the Jaffrey-Fitzwilliam tour.

16.4 **At the fork, the second left at the Woodbound Inn and Woodmere Campground signs, turn sharply left and continue 2.3 miles past the golf course and the Woodbound Inn to a stop sign at a T-junction.**
The Woodbound Inn, a 40-room inn/resort on Contoocook Lake just outside the Jaffrey town line, offers a variety of summer and winter activities, including a par-three public golf course.

18.7 **At the stop sign, turn right onto Squantum Road and ride 0.1 mile to the next left.**

18.8 **Make a hairpin left turn onto Hunt Road (unmarked) and follow it 0.6 mile, when it becomes Contoocook Road and reunites with Squantum Road.**

19.4 **At Squantum Road, merge right and ride 0.6 mile to Howard Hill Road.**
For a swim in Contoocook Lake, make a hairpin left onto Squantum Road for the public beach maintained by Jaffrey.

20.0 **Bear right at Howard Hill Road and ride 0.6 mile to downtown Jaffrey.**

20.6 **You're back where you started.**

Bicycle Repair Services
Andy's Cycle, 165 Winchester Street, Keene (9–6 Mon.–Fri.; 9–5 Sat.; 10–4 Sun., March–Aug.) (352-3410)
Joe Jones Ski and Sport Shop, 222 West Street, Keene (10–9 Mon.–Sat.; 11–6 Sun.) (352-5266)
Norm's Ski and Bike Shop, Martel Court (NH 9/NH 12/NH 101), Keene (10–6 Mon., Tues., Thur., Sat.; 10–9 Fri.; closed Wed. and Sun.) (352-1404)
Roy's Bike and Photo Shop, 58 Main Street, Jaffrey (9–5 Mon.–Fri.; 9–noon Sat.; closed Wed. and Sun.) (532-8800)
Spokes and Slopes, School Street-Depot Square, Peterborough (10–5:30 Mon.–Sat.; till 7:30 Thur.) (924-9961)

6

Greenville-New Ipswich

28.1 miles; challenging cycling
Hilly terrain

The southern New Hampshire towns of Greenville, Temple, and New Ipswich contrast the ways in which economic growth developed in the state during the nineteenth century. Although they are neighbors, each is distinct.

Greenville was an early mill town that prospered in the 1800s when agriculture began to falter and the manufacture of textiles was introduced to this area along the Souhegan River. The textile industry spread and flourished throughout New Hampshire until the 1930s, when most companies moved south. Many of the abandoned red-brick mills lining Greenville's main street were ignored until recent restoration was undertaken for current uses as a public library, an inn, and a restaurant, among others.

The other side of the nineteenth-century industrial revolution is represented in the vintage homes of New Ipswich. Its fine white buildings, most notably Barrett House, are representative of that era. Near Greenville and New Ipswich lies the tiny hilltop town of Temple, whose Grange hall testifies to the dominance of agriculture in its past.

These three towns are connected by a network of secondary roads with light traffic and pleasant views. Since there are several hills to conquer, this tour is suggested as an all-day trip for those who can accept the challenge of some steep hills to earn the rewards of long downgrades.

Two nice old country inns where you might wish to overnight are the Birchwood Inn (878-3285), located on the village green in Temple, and The Ram in the Thicket (654-6440), two blocks off NH 101 in Wilton. Advance reservations are strongly suggested at both inns, especially in July, August, and during foliage season. Dinner at the Birchwood (Tues.–Sat.) is by reservation only. The Ram in the Thicket serves dinner to guests and the public every night and Continental breakfast to guests only, and with some advance notice, it will pack you a box lunch to take with you on your tour.

The tour begins in Greenville at the junction of NH 123 and NH 45 (Main Street and River Street).

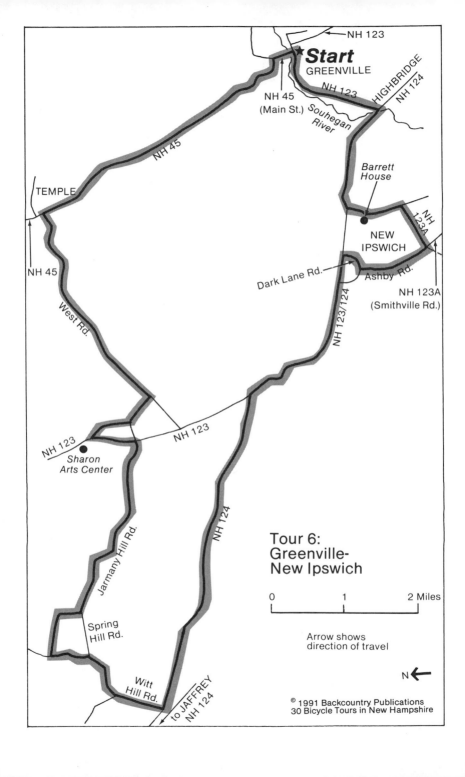

NH 123

★ Start
GREENVILLE

HIGHBRIDGE

NH 123

NH 124

NH 45
(Main St.)

Souhegan
River

Barrett
House

NH 45

NH
123A

NEW
IPSWICH

TEMPLE

NH 45

Dark Lane Rd.

Ashby Rd.

NH 123A
(Smithville Rd.)

West Rd.

NH 123/124

NH 123

NH 123

Sharon
Arts Center

Jarmany Hill Rd.

NH 124

Tour 6:
Greenville-
New Ipswich

0   1   2 Miles

Spring
Hill Rd.

Arrow shows
direction of travel

Witt
Hill Rd.

to JAFFREY
NH 124

N ←

© 1991 Backcountry Publications
30 Bicycle Tours in New Hampshire

0.0   From the junction, proceed north on NH 45 (Main Street) for 0.4 mile, to where NH 45 makes a 90-degree turn to the left up a steep hill.

The red-brick mill structures of Greenville and the old railroad station, which has been converted into the Depot Restaurant, provide a vivid picture of nineteenth-century industrial life.

There are several groceries in the center of Greenville, and of course, you can dine in the Depot Restaurant (11:30–2, 5–9 Wed.–Fri.; 5–10 Sat; 8–11:30, 12–7 Sun.). You also might try the Greenville Inn (878-2761) on the left, just a few yards up Mill Street off Main Street. In continuous operation since 1860, this attractive red-brick inn is open 11:30–9 daily. It also serves Sunday brunch 9–1.

NH 45 is quite narrow as it climbs out of Greenville. However, it runs through a residential area and the traffic generally travels slowly.

0.4   At the turn, follow NH 45 4.0 miles to Temple.

From the top of the hill on NH 45 north of Greenville center you are treated to a fine view of the surrounding mountains.

At the top of the hill, NH 45 widens and the pavement is smooth, although the shoulder is bumpy. Traffic is generally light.

4.4   Just before the cluster of buildings in the center of Temple, turn left onto West Road toward Sharon. Ride for 3.1 miles, always staying on the hard-surfaced road, until you reach a paved road on the right.

From Temple to Sharon, the roads are typical of backcountry New Hampshire: narrow, winding, hilly, with overhanging trees, no shoulders, frost heaves, and very little traffic.

In Temple you can buy food at the general store (7:30–6 Mon.–Sat., 10–1 Sun.), adjacent to the post office. Birchwood Inn, described earlier, is located on the village green nearby.

7.5   At the junction—there is a "Caution Horses" sign on the left, directly opposite the "Temple-Jaffrey" sign—turn right onto the paved road and cycle for 0.5 mile to a fork.

8.0   At the fork, bear right again and ride 0.6 mile downhill to the junction of NH 123.

If you turned right here, you soon would reach the Sharon Arts Center (on the left side of NH 123), which displays and sells works of art and crafts created by New Hampshire artisans. Its gallery and shop are open all year (10–5 Mon.–Sat., 1–5 Sun.). Classes are conducted year-round.

8.6 **At the NH 123 junction, take a sharp left and head south on NH 123 for 0.7 mile to Jarmany Hill Road.**

NH 123 is a two-lane road with a smooth surface, no shoulder, and moderate traffic.

9.3 **Turn right at Jarmany Hill Road and ride for 3.5 miles to a yield sign. Note that after 2.6 miles, Spring Hill Road enters from the left. Bear right at this junction, staying on Jarmany Hill Road.**

Jarmany Hill Road is a winding, narrow country road. Because traffic is very light, it is ideal for biking.

12.6 **At the yield sign, turn left and ride for 1.4 miles to a reddish-brown cape-style house at the foot of a hill, where the road forks.**

14.0 **At the junction of Witt Hill Road and Old Sharon Road, bear left up a short hill on hard-packed-dirt Witt Hill Road and ride another 0.8**

Photo by Susan Heavey

Barrett House beckons the touring cyclist.

mile to NH 124. You probably will need to walk up the hill since the road is steep and rutted, but the remaining section is generally well graded and ridable.

14.8 **Turn left onto NH 124, which merges with NH 123 in about 3.5 miles, and continue for a total of 7.2 miles to Dark Lane Road, to your right on the outskirts of New Ipswich. Watch for a large building with brown-stained siding on your right at this junction.**
NH 124 is a fairly level, smooth, two-lane road with moderate traffic. For the first mile, its shoulder is gravel, but the roadway then widens with a paved shoulder. After merging with NH 123, the road climbs for 0.7 mile before leveling off. Over this uphill stretch the highway is narrow and the paved shoulder disappears, so be careful. Beyond the hill, the road again has a decent shoulder.
Food is available at the NeWest Mall at 21.8 miles.

22.0 **Turn right onto Dark Lane Road, riding uphill for 0.4 mile to Ashby Road.**
Dark Lane Road is a narrow, lightly traveled country lane.

22.4 **Turn left onto Ashby Road and follow it downhill for 1.0 mile through birch stands, stone walls, and attractive old homes, to NH 123A (Smithville Road).**
An excellent view of the mountains to the north opens just as you turn onto Ashby Road. Further along is Appleton Manor Farm, a well-landscaped horse farm with a winding gas-lit driveway, white-fenced paddocks, and barns.

23.4 **At the intersection with NH 123A, turn left and follow it 1.5 miles through New Ipswich, where you rejoin NH 123/NH 124.**
Take time to enjoy the fine old buildings lining the road into New Ipswich: the Congregational Church, town hall (1817), Friendship Manor, the parsonage, and Barrett House, a Federal-style mansion built shortly after 1800 and furnished with exceptionally fine period pieces. It is open June to October, Tuesday through Saturday 11–5. There is a small admission charge.
Food is available at Phil's Market (7–9 daily) at the junction of NH 123A and NH 123/NH 124.
1808 House Restaurant, directly across the street from Phil's Market in a large old Colonial, is a family-style restaurant open for breakfast, lunch, and dinner all day every day except Monday.
NH 123A is a narrow, winding road through a residential area where most traffic obeys the low speed limit.

24.9 **At the intersection with NH 123/NH 124, turn right and ride 1.6 miles to Highbridge, where the two numbered routes split again.**
New Ipswich Market, on the left side of NH 123/NH 124 0.1 mile after turning on this road, is open all day every day.

NH 123/NH 124 is a smooth-surfaced road with a good shoulder and moderate traffic.

26.5 **In Highbridge, turn left onto NH 123 and ride 1.6 miles back to Greenville through rolling countryside along the Souhegan River.**
B & J's General Store offers food at the junction where NH 123 and NH 124 diverge.

NH 123 has no shoulder, a fair surface, and little traffic.

28.1 **You are back at your starting point in Greenville.**

Bicycle Repair Services
Happy Day Cycle, 237 South Street (NH 13), Milford (10–5:30 Tues., Thur., Fri.; 12–7 Wed.; 10–4 Sat.; closed Sun. and Mon.) (673-5088)
Spokes and Slopes, School Street-Depot Square, Peterborough (10–5:30 Mon.–Wed., Fri.–Sat.; 10–7:30 Thur.) (924-9961)
Roy's Bike and Photo Shop, 58 Main Street, Jaffrey (9–5 Mon.–Fri.; 9–12 Sat.; closed Wed. and Sun.) (532-8800)

7

Hancock-Peterborough-Harrisville

27.2 miles; easy to moderate cycling
Rolling terrain, several hills

This tour connects four communities in the Monadnock Region, from the historic to the high-tech, as it rolls through typical New England villages, past old mills and farms, summer theaters, and a major center of literary and technical publications. It starts in the town of Hancock, named for the man who was president of the Continental Congress, a signer of the Declaration of Independence, and the first post-Revolutionary governor of Massachusetts. Hancock does not flaunt its history or its charm. Known for its most typical New England main street, it brings together in one place the scattered pieces of an elusive past: picket fences, a bandstand on the green, a woodframe school, a meeting house, an inn, and elegant old homes. But here the past has been adapted to modern-day life. Hancock does not appear either contrived or too perfect.

The 1788 meeting house, whose bell was forged in Paul Revere's foundry, has been functioning for 200 years. The Museum of Antiques reinforces the town's ties with earlier times. The Hancock Historical Society (Wed.–Sat. 2–4) is at the junction of NH 123 and NH 137. For wonderful country-inn accommodations and food, try the John Hancock Inn (525-3318) on Main Street (NH 123). In operation since 1789, the inn still caters to hungry and tired travelers. The Salzburg Inn and Restaurant (924-3808) on Steele Road in Peterborough, 1.2 miles west of the junction of Summer Street and Main Street, offers you a choice of a modern motel room or a room in an old inn.

Off the beaten track, about 8 miles north of Peterborough, Hancock is easy to reach via US 202 and then NH 123 West. In Hancock also, look for the Hancock Toy Shop on Main Street, where children's furniture and wooden toys are made. The Village Farm sells apples and cider. Across the street from the John Hancock Inn, the Hancock Cash Market, established in 1878, is your last store for provisions until Peterborough, 7.5 miles away.

The tour begins at the bandstand on the Hancock green. Before you start, consider making a 7.8-mile round-trip side jaunt to the Harris Center for Conservation. At the Hancock bandstand, go left on NH 123 North for 2.4 miles and turn left at the sign for Harris Center; go left again

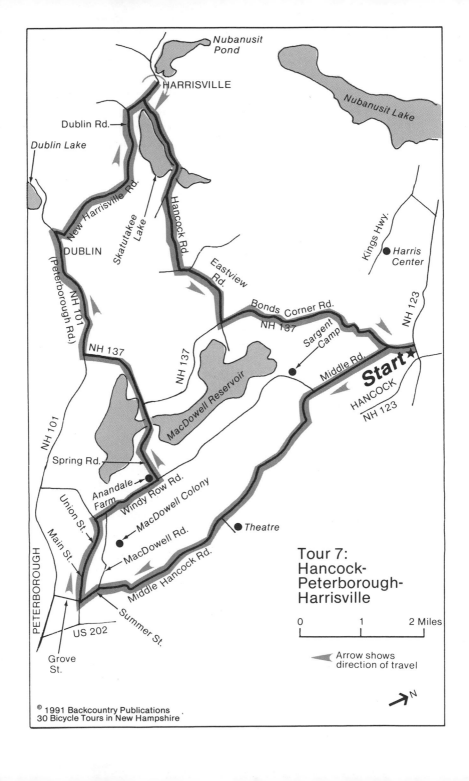

Nubanusit Pond

HARRISVILLE

Dublin Rd.

Dublin Lake

Nubanusit Lake

New Harrisville Rd.

Skatutakee Lake

Hancock Rd.

Kings Hwy.

● *Harris Center*

DUBLIN

Eastview Rd.

NH 101 (Peterborough Rd.)

Bonds Corner Rd.

NH 137

Sargent Camp

NH 123

NH 137

NH 137

Middle Rd.

Start ★

NH 101

MacDowell Reservoir

HANCOCK

NH 123

Spring Rd.

Anandale Farm

Windy Row Rd.

MacDowell Colony

● *Theatre*

Union St.

MacDowell Rd.

Main St.

Middle Hancock Rd.

PETERBOROUGH

Summer St.

US 202

Grove St.

Tour 7:
Hancock-
Peterborough-
Harrisville

0   1   2 Miles

◄ Arrow shows
direction of travel

↗ N

© 1991 Backcountry Publications
30 Bicycle Tours in New Hampshire

at 2.9 miles at Nubanusit Lake and another sign for Harris Center; turn onto a dirt road, King's Highway, and go to the center at 3.9 miles. Backtrack to NH 123, and turn right for return to Hancock.

0.0   From the bandstand on the green, go right on NH 137 South for 0.3 mile, down a steep hill. You reach Middle Road on the left, shortly after the road levels, by what must be the tiniest directional sign in New Hampshire, for Sargent Camp.

NH 137 is narrow but smooth, with no shoulder and light traffic.

0.3   At the Sargent Camp sign, turn left and follow Middle Road, which runs past nicely maintained old farms and homes interspersed with woods, for 7.3 miles to Main Street in Peterborough. At 5.4 miles the road forks and changes its name to Middle Hancock Road. Stay on this road, which at Peterborough changes its name yet again—one of the vicissitudes of New England's geographers—and becomes Summer Street.

About 1.5 miles from the junction of Middle Road and NH 137, a right turn would take you to Sargent Camp, a year-round outdoor education center operated by Boston University. Open to the public (for a nominal fee), it offers hiking, fishing, swimming, overnight lodging and meals (525-3311). At 4.1 miles, a left turn would lead you to the Peterborough Players summer stock theater (924-7585).

Like NH 137, Middle Road is narrow with little traffic, but its surface is not as smooth over rolling-to-hilly terrain, with a one-mile gradual climb and several short descents.

7.6   At the intersection of Summer Street and Peterborough's main street, turn right onto Main Street and head up a short steep hill (where the name changes to Union Street!) for 1.7 miles past the Peterborough playground, to Windy Row Road on the right.

Peterborough, a turn-of-the century New Hampshire town, and the setting for Thornton Wilder's *Our Town,* developed from a frontier settlement in the eighteenth century into a manufacturing community of lumber, woolen, and cotton mills. Now with a population of 5,200, it has become a regional commercial and cultural center. Peterborough established the nation's first free, tax-supported library. The Lyceum, a cultural lecture series originating in the early nineteenth century, continues to be a summer fixture.

Headquartered at Peterborough are Eastern Mountain Sports (EMS) (9–6 Mon.–Sat., noon–6 Sun.), a large outdoor equipment retailer (including bicycling accessories); The Brookstone Company (9–5 daily), retail and mail-order specialists in well-designed tools and high-tech household items; plus several publishers of computer, technical, scientific, and hi-fi magazines. EMS and Brookstone can be reached by turning left at Main Street and left

Photo by Adolphe Bernotas

A summer afternoon break on a New Hampshire village green.

again on U.S. 202. Both are 2.7 miles from Main Street in a well-manicured industrial park with picnic tables and shade trees.

Peterborough Historical Society on Grove Street, a left 0.1 mile west of the Summer Street and Main Street junction, is open weekday summer afternoons, near The Folkway, a New England mecca for folk music on Friday and Saturday nights (lunch and dinner every day, except Monday, and Sunday brunch). Peterborough has several food stores and restaurants, including the A&P, open 24 hours Monday through Saturday and 8–6 Sunday, at the Peterborough Plaza, junction of US 202 and NH 101.

Main Street/Union Street is wide with a good surface, rough shoulder, moderate traffic, and one steep but short grade.

9.3   Turn right onto Windy Row Road and climb gradually past several handsome homes and farms with splendid views of the 2,280-foot Pack Monadnock to the east. In 1.2 miles, just beyond Anandale Farm, you come to Spring Road on the left.

The MacDowell Colony, a 450-acre retreat for writers, sculptors, painters, poets, and composers, is on MacDowell Road, off Windy Row Road. Founded by the wife of composer Edward MacDowell in 1907, it is the country's oldest colony for the arts and presents the prestigious annual MacDowell Medal to artists making outstanding contributions to American culture. MacDowell medalists have included William Styron, Georgia O'Keeffe, Leonard Bernstein, Alexander Calder, John Updike, Elliott Carter, Aaron Copland, Robert Frost, Norman Mailer, Isamu Noguchi, Samuel Barber, and Martha Graham.

Windy Row Road has a fair surface with some frost heaves, no shoulder, but light traffic.

10.5   At Spring Road, turn left and ride 1.3 miles, mostly downhill, to NH 137 just across the Dublin line.

The Game Preserve on Spring Road is a mini-museum displaying more than 700 early American board and card games. Spring Road has a fair surface with some frost heaves and no shoulder.

11.8   At the junction with NH 137, merge left and follow NH 137 for 3.6 miles to NH 101 (Peterborough Road).

Chartered as Monadnock in 1749, it was incorporated in 1771 as Dublin, after Ireland's capital. At 1,493 feet, Dublin is one of New Hampshire's three highest communities. Its Dublin Lake and 3,166-foot Mount Monadnock, the region's highest peak, attract thousands of boaters, swimmers, and hikers every year. Dublin is home to *Yankee* magazine and the venerable *Old Farmer's Almanac,* the nation's oldest continuously published periodical since 1792.

For food, the Dublin General Store is at 14.7 miles.
Although uphill, NH 101 has a smooth, wide shoulder.

15.4 **At the Dublin Fire Department, turn right on New Harrisville Road (which soon becomes Dublin Road) and ride 3.6 miles to Harrisville.**

The surface of New Harrisville Road/Dublin Road is typical New Hampshire backcountry, with frost heaves, no shoulder, and little traffic, but it presents 2.5 miles of scrumptious downhill, followed by a short steep climb into the village of Harrisville.

At 16 miles, looking out from the Dublin School South Slope Ski Area, you get a privileged panorama of the Monadnock Region.

19.0 **You're in Harrisville.**

This town is a museum of a wool-mill community of the industrial revolution in New England. It is named after the Harris family, which built its eloquent red-brick structures, and it is now considered one of the most perfectly preserved mill villages in the nation. Explore

Harrisville is New Hampshire's "Old Mill Stream" community.

this hamlet, reflected in the Contoocook River and Nubanusit Pond. If you stop at Harrisville Designs, a wool-spinning operation, its proprietors will give you a walking tour map.

19.0 After taking in Harrisville, retrace your route for 0.1 mile to the Harrisville General Store.

19.1 From the store, ride down a steep hill, with the Town Selectmen's Office on your right, for 0.1 mile to Dublin Road.

19.2 Turn right onto Dublin Road, then almost immediately left onto Hancock Road, where a hand-painted wooden road sign is nailed to a maple tree, and ride 4.4 miles to NH 137.

Stay on the main road. If you find yourself on dirt, you made a wrong turn. At 20.1 miles, stay left at the fork. At 21.0 bear left at the fork. At 22.5 miles, immediately after a bridge, stay to the right.

Skatutakee Lake, a local fishing hot spot, is at 19.8 miles. Hancock Road (whose name changes to Eastview Road) is shady and windy, a typical backcountry New Hampshire road with very little traffic and delightful downhills.

23.6 At the Junction of NH 137 North, turn left and continue for 3.6 miles to the bandstand, where you started.

NH 137 is bicycling-friendly, with a smooth surface and little or no shoulder, and it glides downhill, with the exception of a steep grade up about 0.3 mile before the end of the tour.

27.2 You're back at the bandstand and your trip is over.

Bicycle Repair Services

Andy's Cycle, 165 Winchester Street, Keene (9–6 Mon.–Fri.; 9–5 Sat.; and 10–4 Sun. March–Aug.) (352-3410)

Joe Jones Ski and Sport Shop, 222 West Street, Keene (10–9 Mon.–Sat.; 11–6 Sun.) (352-5266)

Norm's Ski and Bike Shop, Martel Court (NH 9/NH 12/NH 101), Keene (10–6 Mon., Tue., Thur., Sat.; 10–9 Fri.; closed Wed. and Sun.) (352-1404)

Roy's Bike and Photo Shop, 58 Main Street, Jaffrey (9–5 Mon.–Fri.; 9–12 Sat.; closed Wed. and Sun.) (532-8800)

Spokes and Slopes, School Street-Depot Square, Peterborough (10–5:30 Mon.–Sat.; till 7:30 Thur.) (924-9961)

Summers Backcountry Sports, 16 Ashuelot Street, Keene (9–7 Mon.–Wed.; 9–9 Thur.–Fri.; 9–7 Sat.; 11–4 Sun.) (357-5107)

8

Pierce Homestead–Hillsboro Center

19.8 miles; moderate cycling
Rolling to hilly terrain, several hills

Lovewell Mountain, fourth-highest peak in southern New Hampshire, provides a graceful backdrop for this Currier and Ives tour. But perhaps the most enticing aspect of the trip is the absence of commercial tourism. You can wind unhurriedly along lightly traveled byways and become enveloped by the constantly changing landscape around you — dairy farms with open pasture, thick forests, restored homes set in rural quietude, and small villages with long histories. Recommended as an all-day tour for flower-pickers and picnic-lovers, this trip can also be completed in a half-day spurt.

There are several places nearby where you can enjoy pleasant accommodations. The Stonebridge Inn (464-3155) on NH 9, 1.3 miles east of the junction of NH 9 and NH 31, is a new, little-old country inn with four recently decorated guestrooms. Lunch and dinner are served daily except Monday. Victoria Prewitt's Stonewall Farm Bed and Breakfast (478-5205), on Black Pond Road in Windsor, 1.1 miles from William's Store, provides another very pleasant overnight stay. The Brookwood Motel (478-5258) is located at the junction of NH 9 and NH 31.

The recommended starting point is the Franklin Pierce Homestead, near the intersection of NH 9 and NH 31, 3 miles west of Hillsboro. A polite request for permission to park generally results in an affirmative reply from the manager.

0.0   From the Franklin Pierce Homestead, travel north on NH 31 for 1.9 miles to a fork in the road. Just before the fork there is a dark brown house with attached barn and a signpost for East Washington on the right.

The Franklin Pierce Homestead is the family home of the fourteenth president of the United States. The house, tastefully decorated and furnished with period antiques, is open 10–5 Friday, Saturday, Sunday, and holidays from Memorial Day to Labor Day. A small admission fee is charged. Tatewell Gallery (478-5755), selling antiques and collectibles, is located adjacent to the Pierce Homestead.

Manahan Park, operated by the Town of Hillsboro, is located

Tour 8:
Pierce Homestead-Hillsboro Center

0   1   2 Miles

Arrow shows direction of travel

N

▲ *Lovewell Mtn.*

EAST WASHINGTON

Pond

Coolidge Rd.
(East Washington Rd.)

● *Crane Auction Barn*

Loon Pond

HILLSBORO CENTER

Fox St. Forest

Start

Franklin Pierce Homestead

★

NH 31

HILLSBORO

NH 9

Sawmill Rd.

NH 9/31

Power Station

US 202

Franklin Pierce Lake

© 1991 Backcountry Publications
30 Bicycle Tours in New Hampshire

0.5 mile west on NH 9. It offers a beach and swimming on Pierce Lake.

The Corner Store (7–10 daily) is at the intersection of NH 9 and NH 31. In addition to groceries, it has a very small deli and a counter where you can buy hamburgers and sandwiches. Diamond Acres, on NH 9 across the street from Manahan Park, is a popular drive-in and snack bar open daily during the summer. William's General Store, 1 mile north on NH 31, is open daily, with shorter hours on Sundays (8–1). This is the last store until Hillsboro, 16 miles away.

Photo by Mike Rounds/NH Office of Vacation Travel

HOUSE TOURS
ADULTS $2.00
UNDER 18 FREE

The Hillsboro tour starts from the Pierce Homestead, home of the nation's fourteenth president.

Just a few yards beyond William's Store on the left is Black Pond Road. If you turn left and ride 1.1 miles, you will come to Stonewall Farm Bed and Breakfast.

NH 31, which recently has been reconstructed, is rolling and narrow, and has no shoulder. The road surface is old but quite ridable. Traffic is generally light.

1.9   At the fork bear right toward East Washington and continue for 3.3 miles to a T-junction.

This section of road is known as Coolidge Road on town maps, but it is more commonly referred to as the East Washington Road. Country auctions are held frequently at Crane's Auction Barn, 1.8 miles from the junction of NH 31 and Coolidge Road.

At Lachut's Farm you can watch prize Holsteins grazing. Several antique shops along the way welcome browsers.

Coolidge Road is narrow but generally has a fair surface. The terrain is rolling for about 2 miles, followed by one long downgrade.

5.2   At the T-junction, there are two brown signs, one pointing to Hillsboro Center, the other to East Washington, your destination. Turn left and ride 2 miles through a scenic valley to the village of East Washington.

East Washington, with towering Lovewell Mountain mirrored in its calm pond, impresses the traveler with its serenity.

The 2-mile stretch through the valley has no shoulder and many frost heaves but, on the positive side, very little traffic.

7.2   From East Washington, retrace your route for 2 miles to the T-junction. Proceed straight for 4 miles to Hillsboro Center.

This is a narrow country road with a cracked and bumpy surface. Again, very light traffic provides freedom for the cyclist. After 1.8 miles the road begins a gradual rise that continues for 2.2 miles to Hillsboro Center. The last 0.3 mile is very steep.

Hillsboro Center is a small, picturesque community and historic district. Among its early churches and houses stands the 1773 homestead of its first minister. Although these buildings are not open to the public, their antiquity makes them of interest to the passerby.

Facing the common as you enter the village, take your first right and stop at the brick colonial house with a sign advertising pewter. A retired clergyman makes interesting and reasonably priced pewter. Then return to the main road.

13.2   From Hillsboro Center, continue on the same road for another 3.5 miles to the junction of NH 9 in the town of Hillsboro.

You will pass Fox State Forest, a game refuge and forestry research center, laced with a network of hiking trails. Open farmland below Hillsboro Center offers spectacular views of the mountains of southern New Hampshire.

This stretch of road is somewhat wider and smoother, although it still should be considered secondary. This is all downgrade, the longest coast of the day. Traffic is light.

16.7 **In Hillsboro, turn right and ride 1.7 miles on NH 9 to a paved road by a brick power station at the base of a long hill on your left.**
Since Hillsboro is the commercial center of the area, stores and restaurants provide food and drink.

NH 9 is a major east-west route and consequently requires

The backcountry roads in the Hillsboro area are ideal for family bicycling.

Photo by Susan Heavey

careful cycling. While the speed limit is low, traffic can be moderate to heavy, and the shoulder is narrow.

18.4 **By the power station, turn left onto the unmarked paved road (Saw Hill Road) and follow it for 1.4 miles to the intersection of NH 9 and NH 31.**

Saw Hill Road is a return to narrow, bumpy road conditions with very little traffic.

19.8 **Cross NH 9 back to NH 31 and you quickly return to the Franklin Pierce Homestead.**

Bicycle Repair Services

Bob's Sportshop, 37 Main Street, Newport (9–6 Mon.–Thur. and Sat.; 9–7 Fri.) (863-2734)

Ped'ling Fool, 77 West Main Street, Hillsboro (10–1 Mon., Tue., Thur., Fri.; 9–6 Sat.) (464-5286)

9
Crotched Mountain-Colby Hill (Two-Day Tour)

The distance, difficulty, and terrain appear at the beginning of each day's directions.

Bicycling is easily adapted to personal tastes, desires, and attitude— from an evening ride around the block to an extended cross-country tour. Only the imagination limits the simple, nonpolluting bicycle as a source of recreation and adventure. For variety, couple an active day of cycling with an overnight stay in the inviting atmosphere of an old New England inn. Each inn has a character its own, molded by the personalities of many generations of New Hampshire innkeepers and the weathering of New England seasons. Expect the floors to slant and the stairs to creak, for these are signs of endurance and endearment. After a day of riding, a hot bath, a home-cooked dinner, and a warm bed, you feel as if you have come to visit with an old friend in the country.

This tour offers inns with such warmth and welcome: The Inn at Crotched Mountain in Francestown (588-9694); Colby Hill Inn in Henniker (428-3281); and the Meeting House Inn and Restaurant, also in Henniker (428-3228), at the base of Pat's Peak Ski Area. Conveniently accessible to each other by bicycle, these inns are joined by a network of roads through small towns and appealing countryside. We have designed this trip for the weekend cyclist who seeks to combine a healthy dose of moderate exercise with the peacefulness of a friendly hearth.

We suggest you start at The Inn at Crotched Mountain, adjacent to Crotched Mountain Ski Area, off NH 47, 3.6 miles north of Francestown. The Inn is an old rambling brick-and-wood Colonial. With a spectacular view of southern New Hampshire from the lawn, it sets the perfect tone for your two-day trip. Call ahead for reservations (588-6840 or 588-6841), and plan to arrive in the afternoon or early evening, in time to enjoy the tennis courts and pool. Innkeepers John and Rose Perry go out of their way to provide you with an enjoyable stay.

The Colby Hill Inn, on Western Avenue, 0.5 mile west of its junction with NH 114 in Henniker, is a lovely Colonial house built around 1800. It offers elegant yet comfortable accommodations and dining for its guests and the public (dinner is served every day but Monday and Tuesday).

© 1991 Backcountry Publications
30 Bicycle Tours in New Hampshire

Finish Day One
Start Day Two

Colby Hill Inn

NH 114

HENNIKER

0   1   2 Miles

Arrow shows
direction of travel

N

US 202/NH 9

Western Ave.

covered
bridge

NH 114

The Meeting House
Inn & Restaurant

Pats Peak
Ski Area

HILLSBORO

NH 9

River Rd.

Contoocook River

NH 77

Tour 9:
Crotched
Mountain-
Colby Hill
(2-Day Tour)

WEARE

NH 114/77

SOUTH
WEARE

US 202

NH 114

NH 31

Finish Day Two
Start Day One

ANTRIM

The Inn @ Crotched Mtn.

NH 47

NH 47

NH 77

BENNINGTON US 202/NH 31

US 202

NH 31

Crotched
Mtn.

Mountain
Rd.

Ski Area

FRANCESTOWN

NH 136

NH 13

NEW
BOSTON

NH
136

NH 13 →

Day One
21.8 miles; moderate cycling
Rolling terrain

0.0   **Begin your tour from the Inn at Crotched Mountain by riding 1 mile back to NH 47.**

1.0   **When you reach NH 47, turn left and ride 4.6 miles to Bennington.**
Several antique shops along this route invite browsing. In this part of southern New Hampshire you ride through picture-postcard villages and countryside.

NH 47 is narrow and winding, smooth, with light traffic and no shoulder. Because you are heading away from Crotched Mountain, the land generally slopes downward, making cycling easy.

5.6   **At the junction of NH 31 and NH 47 in Bennington, turn right and ride 0.1 mile to a fork. Bear left and ride another 0.8 mile along the Contoocook River, past the Monadnock Paper Mill to the Junction of US 202.**
If you have time to explore, turn left at the junction of NH 47 and NH 31, and ride 0.1 mile on NH 31 to get to Bennington Country Store (open all day, every day). It offers sustenance for the weary.

Back on the tour just after you take the left fork off NH 31 and NH 47, you come to Alberto's Restaurant, which serves Italian food from 5 PM daily except Sunday.

6.5   **At the junction, turn right onto US 202/NH 31 and ride for 1.7 miles through Antrim, where the numbered highways split.**
Antrim Village Store and Wayno's in downtown Antrim are open all day, every day.

US 202, a major route, is smooth with an intermittent shoulder, good visibility, and generally light-to-moderate traffic.

8.2   **When the numbered highways divide, bear right on US 202 and ride 6 miles to Hillsboro, where US 202 joins NH 9.**
About 1.5 miles beyond Antrim you reach a section of US 202 with a wide paved shoulder, which continues for 3.3 miles.

14.2   **At the junction in Hillsboro, turn right onto US 202/NH 9 and ride 3 miles through town to River Road, on the right.**
Numerous groceries and restaurants are located in Hillsboro. The Stonebridge Inn, a lovely old Colonial structure 0.3 mile west at the junction of NH 9 and US 202, serves lunch and dinner daily except Monday (464-3155).

The section of US 202/NH 9 through Hillsboro has no shoulder and moderate-to-heavy traffic, especially on weekends. However, the speed limit is low and the visibility is good.

17.3 **At the junction of River Road (unmarked), by the sign for West Henniker, turn right and cycle for 4.5 miles to Colby Hill Inn, on your left. River Road is the old Route 202. It crosses the Contoocook River 1.5 miles west of NH 114, and the name changes to Western Avenue.**

River Road has a smooth surface, no shoulder, many curves, and several short, steep hills. Because it parallels the Contoocook River flowing downstream, the riding is generally easy.

21.8 **You are at Colby Hill Inn, your destination for Day One of this tour.**

Day Two
28.2 miles; moderate cycling
Rolling terrain

0.0 **From Colby Hill Inn, continue along Western Avenue, 0.6 mile to the center of Henniker.**

Henniker is home to a covered bridge, as well as to New England College, a small liberal arts school with approximately 1,000 students. Plenty of winter recreation is offered at Pat's Peak, a popular regional ski area, and when the snow melts, outdoor enthusiasts head for The Biking Expedition, Inc., a student bicycle travel program that offers trips in the United States, Canada, and Europe.

Henniker is also home to the New Hampshire Winery, the state's only and New England's first grape winery. For tours and tastings, call 428-9463.

For food and beverages in downtown Henniker, try The Bakery, and Pop Schultz' Market (open all day, every day).

In addition to fine food offered at the Colby Hill Inn and the Meeting House Inn, several other restaurants in Henniker have excellent cuisine. Daniel's Pub (11:30–10:30 Mon.–Sat., 11:30–9 Sun., 428-7621), offers homemade soups, sandwiches, daily specials, and full-course dinners in a pleasant setting overlooking the Contoocook River. Country Spirit Restaurant (11–10 Mon.–Sat., 11–9 Sun., 428-7007), at the junction of NH 9 and NH 113, offers daily specials, full-course dinners, and a bar/lounge.

0.6 **In Henniker, turn right onto NH 114 and continue for 11.3 miles to the junction of NH 114, NH 77, and NH 136, in South Weare.**

Between Henniker and South Weare, several stores are at your disposal, including Country Maid Market at 1.6 miles, Crosby's Store at 7.4 miles, Weare Center Store and Gift Shop at 9.1 miles, and Country 3 Corners at 11.9 miles. With the exception of Weare Center Store, which is closed Monday, all are open all day, every day.

NH 114 is rolling to hilly, with downgrades in your favor. The shoulder varies from one that is wide and paved to nothing at all.

Visibility is generally very good, except for the 2-mile stretch just before the center of Weare. There the road curves over hilly terrain, and we urge caution. While traffic is normally light to moderate, some large trucks do use this route.

11.9 **In South Weare bear right onto NH 77 toward New Boston. In 6 miles, just as you come into the village, you intersect NH 136.**

In New Boston you can buy food at Dodge's General Store (established 1872). To get there from the junction of NH 77 and NH 136, continue south for 0.3 mile to the junction of NH 13. Turn left and ride 0.1 mile to Dodge's. Abigail's bakery, just down the street from Dodge's (across from the library), is excellent.

The Molly Stark Tavern, on NH 13, 0.5 mile south of the junction of NH 77 and NH 136, is an excellent restaurant serving traditional cuisine (lunch, 11:30–2 Wed.–Fri.; dinner 5–9:30 Wed.–Sat. and 1–8 Sun., closed Mon. and Tues.; for reservations call 487-2733).

NH 77 has a good surface but very little shoulder. Normally, traffic is light. The terrain is rolling, generally in your favor.

Photo by Barry Cotter

New Boston's shady village green on the Crotched Mountain-Colby Hill tour.

17.9 **In New Boston, make a hairpin right turn onto NH 136 West and ride 7.2 miles to Francestown.**

One-half mile before the center of Francestown, you pass a historical marker describing a nearby quarry that once yielded high-quality soapstone.

When you turn onto NH 136, you begin a gradual climb that continues all the way back to the Crotched Mountain Inn. It should not present a problem to most cyclists, however. This route is rather curvy with no shoulder and very little traffic.

The Vadney General Store (7–6 Mon.–Sat., closed for lunch noon–1; 9–12 Sun.), is on NH 47 in the center of Francestown.

25.1 **In Francestown, turn right onto NH 47 and cycle 2.6 miles back to the road to the Crotched Mountain Ski Area and the Inn.**

27.7 **At the junction of NH 47 and Mountain Road, turn left to cycle the last mile of your tour.**

28.7 **You are back at the Inn at Crotched Mountain, where you began your two-day tour.**

Bicycle Repair Services

Happy Day Cycle, 237 South Street (NH 13), Milford (10–5:30 Tue., Thur., Fri.; 12–7 Wed.; 10–4 Sat.; closed Sun. and Mon.) (673-5088)

Ped'ling Fool, 77 West Main Street, Hillsboro (10–1 Mon., Tue., Thur., Fri.; 9–6 Sat.) (464-5286)

Spokes and Slopes, School Street-Depot Square, Peterborough (10–5:30 Mon.–Wed., Fri.–Sat.; 10–7:30 Thur.) (924-9961)

Dartmouth–
Lake Sunapee Region

10
Lake Sunapee Loop

23.5 miles; challenging cycling
Rolling to very hilly terrain

With its pine-covered islands, 29 miles of jagged coastline, and crystal water, Lake Sunapee epitomizes the beauty of this rugged part of the Granite State. Mount Sunapee, at 2,743 feet the third-highest peak in southern New Hampshire, rises steeply from the lake's western shore and provides a precipitous backdrop to this popular summer resort area. Because it is a retreat for those who enjoy fishing, swimming, and boating, our tour around the lake is recommended highly for early fall or late spring, the between-season times when snow- and water-lovers are shifting gears.

Indeed, this tour offers you a propitious opportunity to refine your own gear-shifting technique and to test your hill-climbing philosophy. With several long, steep grades to conquer, mind and body are challenged. The tour also provides an opportunity to pit your cycling ability against that of others, for this is the route of the popular Sunapee Bike Race, held annually during the last weekend in August. To try your luck, you can enter the citizens' race. The large numbers of participants are categorized by age: Juniors (18 years and under), Seniors (19 to 29), and Veterans (over 30). Serious racers enter the U.S. Cycling Federation portion of the race and must circle the 22-mile course four times. If the prospect of such intense competition turns you off, take the trip on a cool mid-September day, when you can ride the loop at your own pace.

Because it is a popular resort area, the Lake Sunapee Region has numerous establishments offering dining and lodging. For a map and listing of these places, as well as a listing of the area's attractions, write the Lake Sunapee Business Association, Box 400, Sunapee NH 03782, or call toll-free from outside New Hampshire at 800-258-3530.

Journey's Inn (763-4849) on NH 103B, 1.2 miles from the Sunapee traffic circle, is a good choice for overnight accommodations. Located in a recently restored 200-year-old Colonial, the Inn has private rooms as well as a bunk room for the budget conscious.

Begin your trip at the ski area parking lot in Mount Sunapee State Park, off NH 103 in Newbury. Follow the signs to the rotary by the park entrance, and take the access road 0.7 mile uphill to the base lodge.

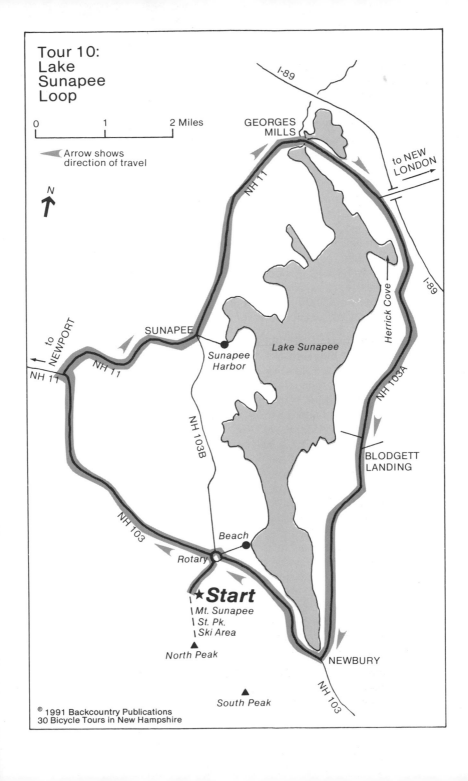

Tour 10:
Lake
Sunapee
Loop

0   1   2 Miles

◄ Arrow shows
direction of travel

N

I-89

GEORGES
MILLS

to NEW LONDON
NEW LONDON

NH 11

I-89

SUNAPEE

to NEWPORT
NEWPORT

NH 11

Sunapee Harbor

Lake Sunapee

Herrick Cove

NH 103A

NH 103B

BLODGETT LANDING

NH 103

Beach

Rotary

★ Start
Mt. Sunapee
St. Pk.
Ski Area

▲ North Peak

▲ South Peak

NEWBURY

NH 103

© 1991 Backcountry Publications
30 Bicycle Tours in New Hampshire

0.0 **From the parking lot, coast 0.7 mile back to NH 103 and turn left on NH 103 West for 4 miles to NH 11.**

Mount Sunapee State Park offers something for everyone. For a nominal admission, you can swim at the sandy beach on Lake Sunapee. A changing house and a lifeguard are provided during the summer. Picnicking, hiking trails, and a gondola to the top of Mount Sunapee are offered at the base of the ski slopes. During the first week in August here, the League of New Hampshire Craftsmen holds its annual fair, the oldest of its kind in the nation. While this is worth attending, it creates unusually high levels of traffic. Consequently, be careful if you plan to cycle this route then.

Snack bars are found at the base and summit lodges. Perkins General Store (7:30–5 daily) is on the right, just north of the Mount Sunapee rotary on NH 103.

NH 103 is a wide two-lane road over rolling and smooth surfaces, with paved shoulder and excellent visibility and generally light-to-moderate traffic. During peak summer weekends the road can be quite busy, however.

4.7 **At the junction of NH 103 and NH 11, turn right onto NH 11 East and ride 7.7 miles to NH 103A, just before the I-89 underpass. Note the sign for Newbury and Blodgett Landing.**

Sunapee Harbor, just off the main route, makes a pleasant rest stop. Turn right at the blinking yellow light on NH 11, 2.5 miles beyond NH 103, and ride 0.5 mile to the water's edge. Should you wish an even closer look at the lake, the MV *Mount Sunapee* offers two cruises daily, at 10:30 AM and 2:30 PM, from late June to Labor Day (763-4030), while the MV *Kearsarge* offers dining cruises at 5:30 and 7:45 during those same weeks (763-5477).

Several food stops are located in Sunapee Harbor. Sunapee Community Store, 0.2 mile from NH 11, is open all day, every day. Woodbine Cottages, across from the marina, serves breakfast, lunch, and dinner and specializes in moderately elegant dining. Georges Mills General Store (open all day, every day), on NH 11 in Georges Mills, 0.5 mile before the junction with NH 103A, is the last place to buy food until you reach Newbury.

Like NH 103, NH 11 is a wide two-lane highway with a smooth surface, paved shoulder, and light-to-moderate traffic along much of the way. The terrain, however, is hillier, including a steep grade just beyond the turn to Sunapee Harbor. Two miles beyond the same turn, the shoulders become intermittent.

12.4 **Following the sign to Blodgett Landing and Newbury, turn right and proceed south on NH 103A for 7.9 miles to its junction with NH 103 in Newbury.**

Watch for the historical marker 0.8 mile south on NH 103A. During the golden age of steamboating on Lake Sunapee, the *Kearsarge, Ascutney, Armenia White,* and others brought hundreds of passengers to this location on Herrick Cove. From there they were transported by stage to New London's hotels and boarding houses. A handsome stone barn on the right, 6.2 miles from the junction of NH 11, overlooks the route.

Frostop Snackbar, the Newbury Harbor Restaurant and Pub, and the Lake Sunapee Trading Post General Store are clustered on NH 103 just after you turn off NH 103A onto NH 103. All are open daily during summer months.

NH 103A is narrow, with no shoulder but a smooth surface. While it carries less traffic than NH 103 and NH 11, it has the steepest hills on the trip. But the hills make the countryside scenic, and numerous old summer homes complement the landscape.

20.3 At the junction in Newbury, turn right onto NH 103 West and ride 2.5 miles to the Mount Sunapee rotary.

NH 103 from Newbury to the rotary is rolling and wide, with a smooth surface and a paved shoulder.

22.8 At the rotary, turn left and climb 0.7 mile back to the parking lot and your car.

Photo by Bill Finney/NH Office of Vacation Travel

Sunapee Harbor offers swimming and tour boats.

23.5 Your tour ends here, at the base of Mount Sunapee.

Bicycle Repair Services

Bob's Sportshop, 37 Main Street, Newport (9-6 Mon.-Thur., Sat.; 9-7 Fri.) (863-2734)

Kiernan's Bicycle Shop, Main Street, New London Shopping Center, New London (9-5:30 Mon.-Fri.; 9-5 Sat.) (526-4948)

11

New London Lakes: Two Short Rides

The distance, difficulty, and terrain appear at the beginning of each trip's directions.

It is little wonder that New London long has been a focal point of recreation in the Dartmouth–Lake Sunapee region, for this hilltop town is surrounded by lakes and commands an exceptional view of 2,937-foot Mount Kearsarge. Situated at the northern end of Lake Sunapee, its history as a resort predates the internal combustion engine, going back to an era when trains, steamboats, and carriages delivered summer vacationers from Boston to its inns and hotels. Its main street still has ties to the past, with its fine old Colonials, several inviting inns, and the red-brick-and-mortar buildings of Colby-Sawyer College.

Today, New London is a residential community and a year-round recreational center. Within easy reach of three major ski areas, three state parks, and numerous lakes, it is an ideal place for a holiday.

New London also offers interesting bicycling. We have chosen two short half-day rides so that those wishing to couple cycling with other activities can do so easily. Because they are short, they are particularly suitable for those new to cycle touring. While New London's location on a hilltop means the bicyclist will have to negotiate several steep grades, the climbs should cause no traumatic aftereffects. Those wanting a longer day of riding can combine the two trips in a figure eight, or take the Lake Sunapee Loop (Tour 10).

The most enticing way to approach your holiday here is to combine cycling with an overnight stay at any of the area's several quality inns. The New London Inn (526-4861), near Little Lake Sunapee, offers eight guestrooms in an intimate house with a kitchen renowned for the exceptional food prepared by its innkeeper, Wolf Heinberg. Pleasant Lake Inn (526-6271), which you pass on the Pleasant Lake loop, was converted from a farm to an inn more than 100 years ago. Maple Hill Farm (526-2248), a bed and breakfast at the Newport Road/Otterville Road junction, is a comfortably renovated 1825 New England farm.

Both rides begin in the center of New London at the parking lot across the street from New London Trust and the Citgo Jiffy Mart.

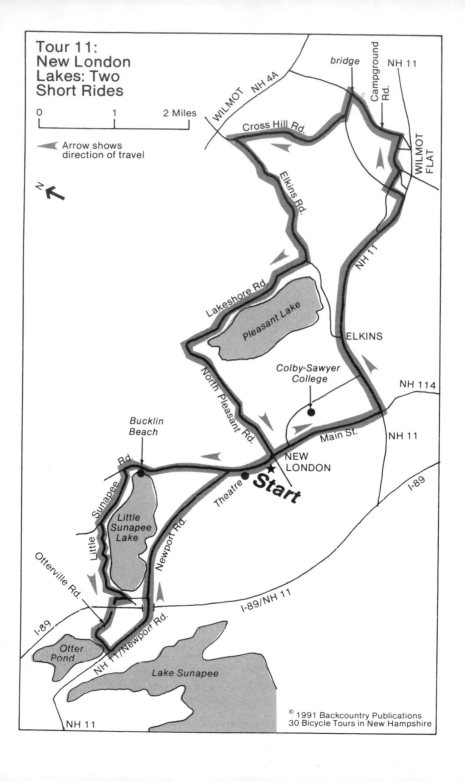

Tour 11:
New London
Lakes: Two
Short Rides

0   1   2 Miles

◄— Arrow shows
    direction of travel

N

WILMOT   NH 4A

bridge

Campground Rd.

NH 11

Cross Hill Rd.

WILMOT FLAT

Elkins Rd.

NH 11

Lakeshore Rd.

Pleasant Lake

ELKINS

*Colby-Sawyer
College*

NH 114

North Pleasant Rd.

Main St.

NH 11

NEW
LONDON

*Bucklin
Beach*

I-89

Sunapee Rd.

*Little
Sunapee
Lake*

Newport Rd.

Theatre

Start

Little

Otterville Rd.

I-89/NH 11

I-89

NH 11/Newport Rd.

*Otter
Pond*

Lake Sunapee

NH 11

© 1991 Backcountry Publications
30 Bicycle Tours in New Hampshire

Little Lake Sunapee
9.6 miles; moderate cycling
Hilly terrain

0.0 **From the parking lot, turn left onto Main Street and proceed for 0.7 mile, passing both the Edgewood Inn (no lodging offered) and the New London Barn Players Theater, to the blinking yellow light, where the road forks.**

New London's Main Street has a variety of shops and well-kept old buildings. Several food stores are available in New London, including the Jiffy Mart at the start of the ride, open all day, every day. Cricenti's is a supermarket on the Newport Road, 1.1 miles northwest of your starting point.

For those who prefer restaurants, try Peter Christian's Tavern (11:30–12:30), in the Edgewood Inn a few blocks north on Main Street. It specializes in hearty soups, salads, sandwiches and quiches. The Millstone on Newport Road is another casually elegant restaurant, open 11:30–2:20 for lunch and from 5:30 for dinner.

Main Street is wide and level with moderate traffic and good visibility.

0.7 **At the fork, bear right and ride 1.4 miles to Little Sunapee Lake.**

The road offers views of the surrounding countryside before it descends to the lakeshore. Bucklin Beach, which you reach about 1 mile from the fork, offers fine swimming during the summer.

The route is a narrow, twisting, two-lane road with a smooth surface and generally light traffic over hilly terrain.

2.1 **At the sharp curve just beyond Bucklin Beach, bear left along the lakeshore, following signs to Springfield and Grantham for 0.8 mile.**

2.9 **When the road starts ascending and curving right, bear left onto Little Sunapee Road, hugging the lakeshore, and ride for 1.6 miles to Otterville Road (unmarked).**

4.5 **At the T-junction you may choose to avoid a somewhat busy hill and a swimming-and-picnicking stop and trim the trip by 1.9 miles for a 7.7-mile loop. For the shorter return, turn right at this T-junction, ride 0.2 mile, then go left on NH 11/Newport Road back into downtown New London.**

For the longer, swim-and-picnic-included ride, turn right and proceed 1.1 miles to Otter Pond, at the junction of Otterville Road and NH 11/Newport Road.

From 2.9 miles to NH 11/Newport Road you ride on narrow, hilly backcountry roads with some frost heaves and limited visibility.

5.6   **At the junction, turn left on NH 11/Newport Road and proceed 0.9 mile past the I-89 interchange and another 2.4 miles to Main Street.**

NH 11/Newport Road is a wide, smooth, two-lane road with paved shoulders, excellent visibility, and moderate traffic.

8.9   **At the Main Street T-junction, turn right for .07 mile to downtown.**

9.6   **You're back at the parking lot where you started.**

Pleasant Lake
14.5 miles; moderate to challenging cycling
Hilly terrain

0.0   **From the parking lot opposite New London Trust, turn right onto Main Street and cycle for 1.6 miles past the New London Inn and Colby-Sawyer College on your left, to the traffic light where Main Street intersects with NH 11.**

Colby-Sawyer College, founded in 1837, enrolls around seven hundred students and offers degrees in liberal arts and medical technology. As you coast down to the intersection of Main Street and NH 11, a panoramic view of Mount Kearsarge and adjacent mountains unfolds—a prelude to what you see on the fantastic downgrade on the next stretch to Wilmot Flat.

In addition to stores and restaurants already mentioned, you pass the Grey House (11:30–9 daily) at the junction of Main Street and NH 11. It offers everything from ice cream cones to full-course dinners.

Main Street is wide with good visibility, moderate traffic, and an intermittent shoulder. Exercise caution on the steep downgrade just before the junction.

1.6   **At the intersection, turn left onto NH 11 East and glide downhill 3.8 miles to the turnoff for Wilmot Flat.**

The views of Kearsarge and surrounding mountains are breathtaking.

NH 11 along this downhill section is a wide two-lane road with good visibility and an excellent paved shoulder.

5.4   **At the turnoff, turn left and ride for 0.1 mile to a T-junction in Wilmot Flat.**

The roads from Wilmot Flat back to New London are generally narrow, curvy, and hilly, with poor visibility but very low traffic. Their surfaces vary from relatively smooth to bumpy with some frost heaves.

5.5   At the T-junction in Wilmot Flat, turn right and ride 0.1 mile past the post office to the intersection with Campground Road.

5.6   At the intersection, turn left onto Campground Road, heading in the direction of Wilmot, and proceed for .08 mile past a narrow bridge.

6.4   Just beyond the one-lane bridge, turn left onto Cross Hill Road and ride 0.2 mile to a fork. Take the right fork and continue up a long gradual hill for 1.7 miles to the intersection of Elkins Road (unmarked), where there is a sign for New London pointing left, "Rocky Acres," and a cluster of four birches.

8.3   Turn left onto Elkins Road, heading for New London, and ride 2.1 miles to a fork in the road.

10.4   At this fork turn right onto Lake Shore Road and continue for 2.5

Part of the fun of touring in New Hampshire is encountering the unexpected–in this case a huge yard sale.

miles. The road will bear to the left as it becomes North Pleasant Road. Follow this road another 1.6 miles back to your starting point.

From the Pleasant Lake Inn, you are treated to a great view of the lake. A historical marker near the inn recounts the exploits of the Pleasant Street Pioneers.

Contrary to its name, North Pleasant Road is very steep, and its grade and roughness demand profound alertness, caution, and pedaling effort. (You may decide to walk!)

If you continue straight instead of turning right onto Lake Shore Road, you come in 0.3 mile to a small store in Elkins.

14.5   Your tour ends on Main Street in the center of New London.

Bicycle Repair Services

Bob's Sportshop, 37 Main Street, Newport (9–6 Mon.–Thur., Sat; 9–7 Fri.) (863-2734)

Kiernan's Bicycle Shop, Main Street, New London Shopping Center, New London (9–5:30 Mon.-Fri.; 9–5 Sat.) (526-4948)

New England Bicycling Center at the Inn at Danbury, NH 104, Danbury Center (12–6 Wed.–Sun.) (768-3318)

12

Canaan-Newfound Lake

54.7 miles; challenging cycling
Rolling to hilly terrain

Here is a trip for those primarily interested in a full day of challenging cycling. It has two possible starting points—Canaan if you make it a day trip, or Danbury if you want a two-day adventure and an overnight in rural New Hampshire. Bounded by the communities of Plymouth, Franklin, and Enfield, the rural area this tour circles until recently has been forgotten by tourists and developers attracted to the more glamorous Seacoast, Lakes and White Mountain regions. People are beginning to discover its clear lakes, rushing streams, and formidable mountains. While growth extending east from Hanover and west from Plymouth and Franklin may one day change this part of New Hampshire, for the immediate future it is an excellent place to enjoy long-distance rural cycling. Suggested for the more experienced cyclist, the ride offers long stretches for the quiet unity of man and machine to relish the pace and rhythm of uninterrupted movement. With the exception of the stretch along the western shore of Newfound Lake, you encounter little traffic. Unlike most of our other tours, this one does not offer numerous historic or architectural points of interest. Its beauty is in waterfalls, sculpted rocks, and other natural phenomena.

Several inns and bed-and-breakfast establishments are on or near the route. Canaan offers The Inn on Canaan Street (no smoking) on one of the most beautiful streets in the state, planned in 1788 (523-7310); and The Towerhouse Inn, at US 4 and NH 118 at the base of 3,121-foot Mount Cardigan (523-7244). Six Chimneys Bed and Breakfast (744-2029), on NH 3A in East Hebron, is a lovely 1790 Colonial, once used as an eighteenth-century coach stop. The owners, Mr. and Mrs. Peter Fortescue, lived in England and Spain and have decorated the house with antiques from both countries. A large and tasty breakfast is another highlight for cyclists who stay here—especially since it is nine miles to any other food. The Inn at Danbury (768-3318), on NH 104, 0.3 miles from Danbury Center, is suited perfectly to the cyclist because in addition to the inn, it operates a bicycle shop from mid-May through October.

For the day trip, begin in Canaan at the junction of US 4 and NH 118, easily accessible from I-89. If you wish a two-day trip with an overnight stay at a rural inn, start at the Inn at Danbury at mile 40.2, and continue the tour clockwise.

0.0 **From Canaan, head north on NH 118 for 8.2 miles to paved River Road, on the right. This road is about 0.2 mile beyond the dirt crossroad that leads on the right to Province Road State Forest. If you find yourself in the tiny village of Dorchester, you have ridden too far on NH 118.**

The turnoff for Cardigan State Park is approximately 0.5 mile north of Canaan on NH 118. While the park offers picnicking and hiking trails, we don't recommend the detour unless you have plenty of time and energy. It is a 4-mile ride, sometimes uphill, into the park, and another 4 miles back out. If you're bounding with energy, you may wish a shorter side trip to Cilley's Cave, where a hermit lived for nearly 40 years. To get there, take the road to Cardigan State Park only as far as the town hall in Orange, then hike up the Orange Pond Trail, which starts behind the town hall.

Evans Express Mart (523-7578) and Jesse's Market (523-4833) — both on US 4 — and Canaan Cash Market (523-4362) on Depot Street are three places for food in Canaan. All three are open all day, seven days a week. The neighborhood also offers the Shiny Plate Restaurant.

NH 118 is a two-lane road with an adequate biking surface and gravel shoulder. It is fairly level as you leave Canaan, but you encounter some hills as you go farther north.

8.2 **Turn right at River Road and proceed along Baker River for 4.3 miles until you rejoin NH 118.**

As you enjoy the pleasant downgrade along Baker River's east side, keep an eye out for waterfalls and cascades.

River Road, although paved, is narrow and rough with virtually no traffic.

12.5 **When you reach NH 118, turn right and ride for 0.9 mile to a four-way intersection at the foot of a hill (approximately 0.5 mile beyond the Dorchester General Store).**

The Dorchester General Store (8:30–8:30 daily, closed Mon. and Tues., 786-9222) offers a restaurant, supplies, home-baked muffins, and outstanding hospitality. It is your last opportunity to buy food until Hebron, 11 miles farther on.

This stretch of NH 118 is similar to the previous segment.

13.4 **At the junction, turn sharply right and ride 3.8 miles toward Groton. The sign for Groton, on the right, is easy to miss.**

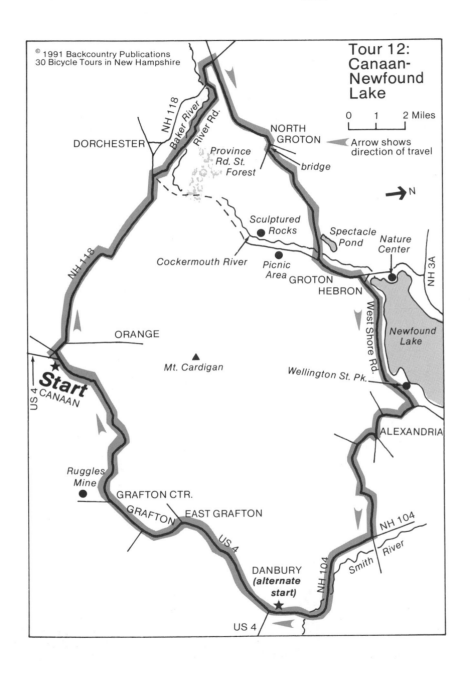

© 1991 Backcountry Publications
30 Bicycle Tours in New Hampshire

Tour 12:
Canaan-
Newfound
Lake

0   1   2 Miles

Arrow shows
direction of travel

→ N

NH 118

Baker River

River Rd.

DORCHESTER

Province
Rd. St.
Forest

NORTH
GROTON

bridge

Sculptured
Rocks

Spectacle
Pond

Nature
Center

NH 3A

Cockermouth River

Picnic
Area

GROTON

HEBRON

NH 118

ORANGE

Mt. Cardigan

Newfound
Lake

West Shore Rd.

Start

US 4

CANAAN

Wellington St. Pk.

Ruggles
Mine

GRAFTON CTR.

GRAFTON

EAST GRAFTON

US 4

ALEXANDRIA

NH 104

Smith River

NH 104

DANBURY
*(alternate
start)*

US 4

This road is a narrow country byway with no shoulder, very little traffic, and generally a rough surface. Over the first 1.9 miles you climb, sometimes steeply; then for the next 1.8 miles you descend through pleasant, open countryside.

17.2   At the fork at the bottom of the hill in North Groton, follow the main road as it heads to the right over a short bridge toward Groton, 4.8 miles away.

The road continues as a narrow byway with a generally rough surface. You climb again for 0.9 mile but are rewarded with a delicious and often steep descent 3 miles long. The last 0.9 mile to Groton is fairly level.

22.0   At the intersection in Groton, turn sharply left to stay on the main road and ride 1.6 miles. Note the sign for Wellington State Park and Bristol pointing in your direction of travel.

You ride through reasonably level valley farmland to Hebron.

If you turn right at the intersection in Groton onto the minor road and ride 1.1 miles, you come to Sculptured Rocks Geologic Site, part of the New Hampshire Division of Parks. Glaciers have sculptured potholes and rocks in the Cockermouth River that make per-

A break at Wellington State Park on the Canaan-Newfound Lake tour.

Courtesy Fred McLaughlin/Haggett's Bike Shop, Concord

fect sliding and swimming platforms. Walking trails along the river and plenty of places to picnic abound.

23.6 At the village green in Hebron, turn right onto West Shore Road for 5.7 miles along Newfound Lake to a stop sign.

Hebron is a pretty New Hampshire town with a schoolhouse, church, and general store fronting a gas-lighted green. If instead of turning right you continue straight for about 1 mile through Hebron, staying to the right of the green, you come to Paradise Point Audubon Nature Center at the northern end of Newfound Lake. It features natural history, environmental, and wildlife exhibits, nature walks, and films. The Center is open daily from the last week in June through Labor Day 10–5. A donation of $1 for adults and $.50 for children is requested. One mile beyond the nature center, at the junction of NH 3A, is Six Chimneys Bed and Breakfast (described earlier) where, if you have changed your mind about making this a one-day tour, you might want to stop, making this a leisurely two-day tour.

Wellington State Park, to your left on West Side Road 4.4 miles south of Hebron, is a welcome spot for cyclists. The park offers swimming in Newfound Lake, picnicking, and 12 hiking trails should you desire a respite.

Hebron Village Store, adjacent to the green, is open all day, every day, and sells sandwiches and groceries.

West Shore Road is a narrow two-lane road over rolling-to-hilly terrain with limited visibility. In summer, caution is urged because of traffic.

29.3 At the stop sign, turn right toward Alexandria and follow the main road 1.2 miles.

From West Shore Road to Alexandria and on to NH 104, the roads tend to be typical of backcountry New Hampshire: winding and rolling, with poor-to-fair surface and no shoulders.

30.5 Turn sharply left by the sign for Alexandria and ride past the town hall and the Alexandria Volunteer Fire Department for 1.3 miles.

31.8 At the fork, bear left onto the bumpy road and ride 4.1 miles to NH 104.

35.9 At NH 104, turn right and ride along the river 4.6 miles to US 4 and the center of Danbury.

NH 104 is a wide road with paved shoulders for 2.5 miles, good visibility, and fast traffic. The remaining 2 miles offer a good surface, but the shoulder turns to gravel and the roadway tends to be curvy.

The Inn at Danbury with its bicycle shop, described in the introduction to this tour, is at 40.2 miles on the right.

40.5 **In Danbury, turn right onto US 4 and bike for 14.2 miles through the Graftons back to Canaan.**

Because US 4 is fairly open, you have good views of the countryside and mountains. The road to the Ruggles Mine, an old mine worth visiting, leaves from Grafton Center (there's a sign to direct you). However, we suggest you avoid its steep grades on your bicycle. The road is very narrow and poorly surfaced, and the side trip is better made by car. The Grafton General Store is on the right, before the Ruggles Mine turnoff.

The junction of US 4 and NH 104 in Danbury has two food stores; Dick's Village Store and Danbury General Store are open all day, every day, as is the C&G Convenience Store, on US 4 in Grafton 7.6 miles from its junction with NH 104.

US 4 is level to rolling, with good visibility, a smooth surface, and a gravel shoulder.

54.7 **You are in Canaan, your starting point.**

Bicycle Repair Services
Kiernan's Bicycle Shop, Main Street, New London Shopping Center, New London (9–5:30 Mon.–Fri.; 9–5 Sat.) (526-4948)
New England Bicycling Center at the Inn at Danbury, NH 104, Danbury Center (12–6 Wed.–Sun.) (768-3318)
Omer and Bob's, 7 Allen Street, Hanover (9–6 Mon.–Thur., 9–7 Fri., 9–5 Sat.) (643-3525)
Tom Mowatt Cycles, 3 High Street, Lebanon (9–6 Mon.–Fri.; 9–5 Sat.) (448-5556)
Tom Mowatt Cycles, Olde Nugget Alley, Hanover (9–6 Mon.–Fri.; 9–5 Sat.) (643-3522)

13

Potter Place-Lake Mascoma

57 miles; challenging cycling
Rolling to hilly terrain

An alternative to the Canaan-Newfound Lake tour (Tour 12), this ride repeats about a quarter of that route and takes you over 57 miles of farms, forests, and marshes, making only five turns. All but a half-mile of the ride follows two roads, US 4 and US 4A, superb highways freed up of traffic by I-89 and now left almost forgotten, serving the unhurried bicycling traveler with excellent out-of-the-way country inns. If you are acquainted with Connecticut, the name places of this area will be familiar. The route takes you through Danbury, Wilmot, Andover, Grafton, Enfield, Orange, Canaan, Lebanon, and Springfield—at least four of these places were christened after Connecticut communities. The names were brought from Connecticut by families who were granted tracts in the northern wilderness by New Hampshire's pre-Revolutionary royal governors.

This tour is a half-day workout for the accomplished cyclist or a two-day journey for the more leisurely rider through an area of New Hampshire where development calmed down 20 years ago. It takes you through areas no longer visited by the hurried and harried motorists who bypass this region on I-89. Before the interstate was stretched northwest from Concord, New Hampshire's capital, toward Vermont and Canada in the 1960s, US 4 was the major east-west route in this part of the state and US 4A its alternate, but I-89 vacuumed the cars off these highways and left the roads much more friendly to bicyclists. The roads for the most part are smooth and wide, with good shoulders, good visibility, and little traffic. But they are open, with little shade, and on sunny days this can make for warm cycling, making the route perfect for an overcast day.

About a third of the route is fairly flat, following railroad beds and the northern and southern shores of Lake Mascoma ("Mascoma" being the Algonquin word for water and fish). But the rest is rolling to hilly, with occasional up-grades of 9 percent—and then an equally occasional downslide of 11 percent! Taken briskly, it is a perfect training ride for the more athletically inclined. The Inn at Danbury (no smoking), a bicyclist-friendly place with an indoor heated pool, state-of-the-art exercise equipment, and a bike shop (NH 104 off US 4, 768-3318), is a center for

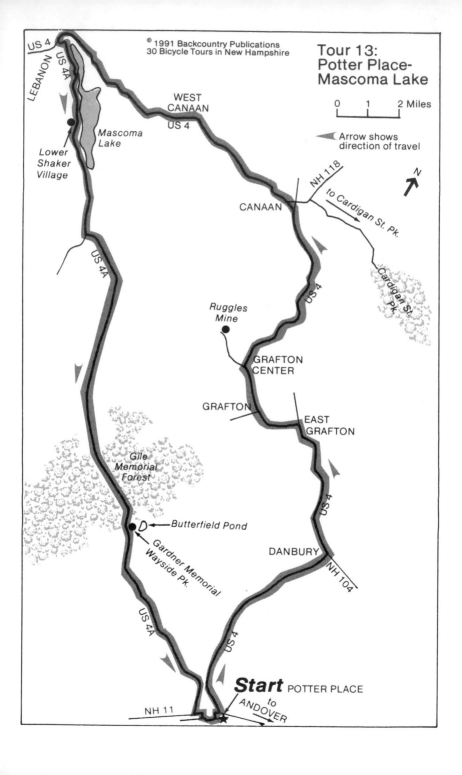

© 1991 Backcountry Publications
30 Bicycle Tours in New Hampshire

**Tour 13:
Potter Place-
Mascoma Lake**

0   1   2 Miles

◀ Arrow shows
direction of travel

N

US 4
LEBANON
US 4A

WEST
CANAAN
US 4

Mascoma
Lake

Lower
Shaker
Village

CANAAN

NH 118

to Cardigan St. Pk.

US 4A

Cardigan St.

Cardigan
Pk.

Ruggles
Mine

US 4

GRAFTON
CENTER

GRAFTON

EAST
GRAFTON

Gile
Memorial
Forest

US 4

Butterfield Pond

Gardner Memorial
Wayside Pk.

DANBURY

NH 104

US 4A

US 4

Start POTTER PLACE

NH 11

to
ANDOVER

training triathaloners and uses this ride as a conditioning jaunt. But don't let that daunt you. As a two-day ride, it yields spectacular scenery, including Mount Kearsarge, Mount Cardigan, and Lake Mascoma, as well as New Hampshire's other (see Tour 18) Shaker community museum at Enfield. The former Shaker colony offers lodging in historic buildings, as well as dining in the "Great Stone Dwelling" at the Shaker Inn and Conference Center on NH 4A (632-7800).

Other accommodations of food, drink, and/or bed are offered in Canaan by The Inn on Canaan Street (no smoking), on one of the most beautiful streets in the state, planned in 1788 (523-7310, 523-9011); and The Towerhouse Inn, at US 4 and NH 118 (523-7244); the English House B & B in Andover (735-5987); and Andover Arms Guest House, NH 11, Andover (735-5953).

The ride starts in the village of Potter Place, about two miles west of the junction of US 4 and NH 11 at Andover, where the Potter Place Restaurant (735-5141) will accommodate you with food.

0.0   **From Potter Place, keeping the railroad station-museum to your left and the post office to your right, head out toward US 4 West and ride for 7.4 miles north to Danbury.**

The village of Potter Place, which contains a former railroad station — now the Andover Historical Society Museum (10–3 Sat., 1–3 Sun., 735-5402) — the post office, and the inn, is named after Richard Potter, a famous magician, ventriloquist, and showman who died at his mansion in Andover in 1835. When his grave had to make way for a Northern Railroad terminal, his remains were moved a short distance away, and the station and village were named in his honor.

Before you have traveled seven miles, you will pass through "artisan alley," encountering a potter, a leather worker, a jeweler, and a chair re-caner.

The road is smooth and open, with only occasional shade and little traffic. The shoulder disappears at about 5.0 miles.

7.4   **In Danbury, at the junction of NH 104, bear left, staying on US 4 West for 24.2 miles to the junction of US 4A in Lebanon.**

Two places for provisions are available at this junction, Dick's Village Store and the Danbury General Store. The Inn at Danbury, with its bike shop, is 0.3 mile up NH 104 on the left.

The road takes you through East Grafton, Grafton, and Grafton Center, past cornfields, marshes, and cemeteries. At 13.5 miles you pass the Grafton Volunteer Fire Department and at 14.9 miles the road for Ruggles Mine, which has been operating since 1803.

The nation's oldest mica, feldspar, and beryl mine is worth a visit for its minerals and its spectacular view of 3,121-foot Mount

Cardigan. But unless you're on a mountain bike, the steep, narrow, and poorly surfaced road is better taken by car than road bike.

The Graftons have two stores, C&G Convenience Store and the Grafton General Store.

At the junction of NH 118 at 21.5 miles into the trip, you reach Canaan and the turnoff for Cardigan State Park, an 8-mile detour for picnicking and hiking. Canaan also has Jesse's Market, Evans Express Mart, and the Shiny Plate Restaurant.

As you head toward West Canaan, at 33.9 miles into the ride on your left is the United Methodist Wayside Chapel, one of the most photogenic church buildings in the area. The area is chronicled at the Canaan Historical Museum on Canaan Street (Memorial to Columbus Day weekends, 1–4 Sat., 523-4202). As you ride out of Canaan, you pass the Pleasant Valley Store and Cathi and Don's Country Store, as well as Tom's Ice Cream and Tinkham's Store.

The road from Danbury to Canaan follows a railway bed, making for generally flat-to-rolling terrain along smooth surfaces and in most places adequate shoulders. Past Canaan, the road becomes hillier and the shoulder widens for about 3 miles after NH 118, then turns to gravel. But you get a downhill of at least 2 miles, then a steep uphill followed by a rewarding downgrade. The ups and downs even out somewhat, and the shoulder improves as you reach Enfield and Lebanon.

31.6 At US 4A in Lebanon, make a hairpin left turn and ride along Lake Mascoma through several towns for 24.5 miles back to Andover.
Keeping serene Lake Mascoma to your left, after about 3 miles you arrive at the Shaker community in Enfield. Explore this remarkable historic colony. You can spend the night and dine at the Shaker Inn, take a guided tour of its museum, other exhibits, and gardens in Lower Shaker Village, or visit the Village Emporium, which offers Shaker furniture reproductions. The Enfield Shakers established themselves in stone buildings along the lake in the early 1800s, one of several colonies of the celibate sect that thrived in New England. It left a legacy of simple and functionally elegant design in objects from furniture to farm implements. (For New Hampshire's other Shaker ride, see Shaker Village-McAuliffe Planetarium, Tour 18).

Some of the village today retains its religious use. Much of it is operated as a Roman Catholic retreat and shrine by the LaSalette Brotherhood of Montreal.

About two miles out of the Shaker village, you pass Mascoma Lake Lodge on the left, and less than a mile farther, Proctor's Store on the right. At 53.1 miles into the trip on the Springfield-Wilmot line, on the left is the Gardner Memorial Wayside Park in the Gile Memorial Forest, where you can picnic near Butterfield Pond and visit an old mill site.

At 55.3 miles into the tour, straight ahead, you are treated to a magnificent view of 2,937-foot Mount Kearsarge.

US 4A initially has a smooth and flat-to-rolling surface, with no shoulder and little traffic. Past the Shaker community, the road rises and falls across the hills, leveling off occasionally.

56.1   At the junction of US 4A, turn left on NH 11 East and ride 0.6 mile to the turn for Potter Place.

You pass the last store on this route, Kearsarge Mini Mart, on the

Courtesy Shaker Inn

The Shaker Inn at Enfield on the Potter Place-Mascoma tour.

left, just after the turn onto NH 11.

The road is wide and smooth, with an excellent shoulder.

56.7   Turn right for Potter Place and ride 0.2 mile to a T-junction.

56.9   At the T-junction turn left and ride 0.1 mile until you run up against a fence.

57.0   Walk your bicycle around the fence, across the railroad tracks, and back to Potter Place, where you started.

Bicycle Repair Services

New England Bicycling Center at the Inn at Danbury, NH 104, Danbury Center (12–6 Wed.–Sun.) (768-3318)

Tom Mowatt Cycles, 3 High Street, Lebanon (9–6 Mon.–Fri.; 9–5 Sat.) (448-5556)

14
Hanover-Orford

36.8 miles; moderate cycling
Rolling terrain

Hanover is the cultural and educational center of northwestern New Hampshire. It is the home of Dartmouth College, the Hood Museum of Art, the Hopkins Center for the Performing Arts, and the Dartmouth-Hitchcock Medical Center. Stately, ivy-covered college buildings, wide lawns bordering tree-lined streets, and the Hanover Inn overlooking an expansive village green lend a feeling of tradition and stability to the town. At the same time, book-laden college students and numerous specialty shops convey excitement and activity.

Yet within five minutes of leaving town, you are cycling amid the farms, pastures, and cornfields of the northern Connecticut River Valley. While such a contrast promotes momentary culture shock, the transition is pleasant. The cycling is generally easy, and the scenery magnificent. The tour is a moderate one. Make it an all-day affair, allotting ample time for exploring the towns of Lyme and Orford.

Also budget time for a picnic lunch along the Connecticut River. Slowly snaking its way among the round-topped hills of eastern Vermont and the foothills of New Hampshire's White Mountains, the valley's serenity is contagious. You'll return to Hanover relaxed, refreshed, and ready for a good dinner to end a perfect day.

Several inns along your route provide warmth and comfort, should you decide to complement your cycling with an overnight stay.

This trip begins at the Hanover Inn, by the Dartmouth College green. While parking spaces are available here, they usually are full, so you may want to head for nearby side streets or municipal lots.

0.0   From the green, follow East Wheelock Street, which is also NH 10, past the Hanover Inn, the Hopkins Center, and the Hood Museum, a couple of blocks to a traffic light. Turn left and stay on NH 10, then turn right at the next traffic light. Continue north on NH 10 for 10.7 miles to Lyme.

In Hanover, Dartmouth College, the Hopkins Center, and the town itself offer numerous activities. For up-to-date information, call the Hopkins Center at 646-2422.

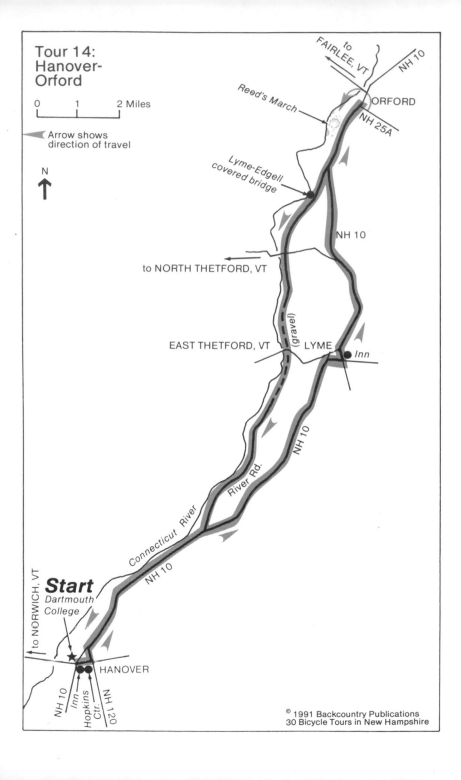

Tour 14:
Hanover-
Orford

0   1   2 Miles

◄ Arrow shows
   direction of travel

N

to
FAIRLEE, VT

NH 10

Reed's March

ORFORD

NH 25A

Lyme-Edgell
covered bridge

NH 10

to NORTH THETFORD, VT

(gravel)

EAST THETFORD, VT

LYME

Inn

NH 10

River Rd.

NH 10

Connecticut River

NH 10

Start
*Dartmouth
College*

to NORWICH, VT

NH 10

HANOVER

Inn

Hopkins
Ctr.

NH 120

© 1991 Backcountry Publications
30 Bicycle Tours in New Hampshire

You can buy food at the Grand Union supermarket (8–9 Mon.–Sat., 8–6 Sun.) on Main Street (NH 10). Groceries and deli food are also available at Pat and Tony's General Store on NH 10, 1.4 miles into the trip.

Hanover has several enjoyable places for dining. Peter Christian's Tavern (11:30–12:30 daily), Molly's Balloon (11–10 Sun.–Thurs.; 11–11 Fri., Sat.) and Delicatessen (8:30–5 Mon.–Sat.), Lai's Restaurant (6:30–3 Mon.–Thurs.; 6:30–9:30 Fri.–Sat.; 8–3 Sun.), and 5 Olde Nugget Alley (11–11:30 Mon.–Sat.; Sun. brunch 10:30–2, dinner 4:30–11) are a few. All four are on Main Street.

The Hanover Inn (643-4300) on the green is an elegant brick building with nicely appointed lobby and rooms. Across the Connecticut River on Main Street in Norwich, Vermont, is the Inn at Norwich (802-649-1132), established in 1797.

NH 10 is wide and smooth, with excellent shoulders. While traffic tends to be considerable in town, it thins out as you head north. The terrain is hilly, but the roadway is well graded, with gradual slopes. Visibility is excellent, providing fine views of the Connecticut River and the mountains and farms of New Hampshire and Vermont.

10.7 **In Lyme, bear sharply right off NH 10 onto the road that edges the right side of the long town common. At the head of the common turn left, in front of the Lyme Inn, and take the road between the church and horse sheds to a yield sign, where you rejoin NH 10. Continue north another 7.3 miles to Orford.**

Lyme's Congregational Church was built in 1812 and its horse sheds are a rare example of original meeting house outbuildings. The Lyme Inn (795-2222), built between 1802 and 1809, is a small, intimate country inn where area literati and artists often gather Sunday afternoons for readings and discussions. It has 15 rooms and serves dinner daily except Tuesday. Reservations for lodging and dinner are suggested.

In Lyme you can buy lunch or a snack at the counter in Nichol's Hardware (7:30–5:30 Mon.–Sat.) or groceries and sandwiches at the Lyme Country Store (8–8 Mon.–Sat., 9–6 Sun.).

After Lyme, NH 10 narrows and the shoulder, when it exists at all, is loose gravel. However, visibility remains excellent and there are fewer hills. While traffic is generally light to moderate, it moves fast; we urge caution.

18.6 **In Orford, at the red-brick churchlike building that houses the Masonic Temple, turn around and retrace your route 2.7 miles to River Road (unmarked).**

In Orford, note the seven "ridge" houses. Built between 1773 and

1839, they display the influence of architects Charles Bulfinch and Asher Benjamin. Orford was also the home of Samuel Morey, credited with inventing American's first marine steam engine, predating Robert Fulton's 1803 boat by nearly 10 years.

The White Goose Inn (353-4812), 0.9 mile south of Orford, is a meticulously refurbished brick structure built in 1833. With its beautifully decorated parlor, guestrooms, and dining room, it creates a special atmosphere for guests who wish to enjoy its bed-and-breakfast accommodations. The innkeepers do not serve lunch or dinner.

Orford is home to Meldrim Thomson, New Hampshire's former feisty governor (1973–79). His family operates Equity Publishing

Photo by Jon-Pierre Lasseigne

The Hanover-Orford tour is among several New Hampshire rides through covered bridges.

Company on the main street, one of the country's premier publishers of law books in English and Spanish. At the family farm by the foot of Mount Cube, about 8 miles to the east on NH 25A, the Thomson hospitality overflows weekends at a tiny restaurant where the state's former first lady, Gale Thomson, serves her famous pancakes with indigenous maple syrup to tourists and presidential politicians.

Food can be bought at Weeks' General Store (8–8 Mon.–Sat., 9–6 Sun.). You won't see any more restaurants or stores until you return to the outskirts of Hanover.

21.3   At the "Antiques 3 mi." sign, turn right off NH 10 and ride 5.3 miles, through the Lyme-Edgell covered bridge, to a stop sign.
Reed's Marsh, a New Hampshire wildlife-management area just south of Orford and adjacent to the Connecticut River, supports a variety of bird, animal, and fish species. The Lyme–Edgell covered bridge, constructed in 1885 by Walter and J.C. Piper, is 154 feet long and crosses Clay Brook. The countryside around this backroad is mostly corn fields and pastureland.

Although the backroads along the river often are cracked and bumpy, they are quite ridable. They are narrow with no shoulders, but have very little traffic. At 3.8 miles after you turn off NH 10, the road turns to gravel for 1 mile. However, it is hard-packed, wide, and level, so it should present no problem.

26.6   At the stop sign and crossroad that leads to the right over the river to Vermont, continue straight 5.5 miles before rejoining NH 10.

32.1   Turn right onto NH 10 and retrace the rest of your route for 4.7 miles back to Hanover.

36.8   You are back at your starting point at the Hanover Inn.

Bicycle Repair Services
Omer and Bob's, 7 Allen Street, Hanover (9–6 Mon.–Thur., 9–7 Fri., 9–5 Sat.) (643-3525)
Tom Mowatt Cycles, Olde Nugget Alley, Hanover (9–6 Mon.–Fri.; 9–5 Sat.) (643-5522)

Concord Area

15

Chichester-Loudon

24.1 miles; easy to moderate cycling
Flat to rolling terrain; one major hill

Tucked away where the Lakes, Seacoast, and Merrimack Valley regions meet, this corner of New Hampshire offers outstanding bicycling within a few minutes' drive of Concord, the state capital. It is also only a couple of hours north of metropolitan Boston, making this ride a fine day trip. The tour can be taken as an adjunct to other tours in this book, especially those in the Concord area.

Historically a farming and maple syrup-producing region, the area also has an honorable mercantile history. The community of Pittsfield thrived as a nineteenth-century industrial center, churned by the mills on the Suncook River. Pittsfield remains the home of the Globe Manufacturing Company, a world-renowned firm specializing in firefighting clothing since 1887. Although the area is surrounded by cities—Concord to the west, Laconia and Franklin to the north, and Rochester somewhat farther to the east—it remains barely touched by metropolitan influences. If the utility poles, occasional satellite dishes, and farm tractors were to be hidden away, the area would easily become a movie set for pre-Edison rural New England, with its dairy and horse farms, orchards, and maple sugarbush operations. Chichester's picture-postcard village center is famous locally for the bean suppers dished out every other Saturday night, May through October, at the United Methodist Church. The ride through Loudon, Gilmanton, and Pittsfield takes you through the communities' more rural parts. (You may wish to avoid this tour during the third weekend in June, when these byways buzz with motorcyclists drawn to the New Hampshire International Speedway on NH 106 in Loudon for the Loudon Classic Motorcycle Races, the oldest of their ilk in the country.) The tour includes flat-to-rolling terrain, but it also has some climbs, the rewards of which are generous panoramas of central and Lakes Region New Hampshire.

If you wish to spend the night here, two bed-and-breakfast establishments are handy, unless you choose to stay in Concord, whose accommodations and attractions are listed in Tour 18. Closer to Chichester, the starting point of this ride, is the Victorian Country Club. This erstwhile farm has been turned into a combination bed and breakfast, restaurant,

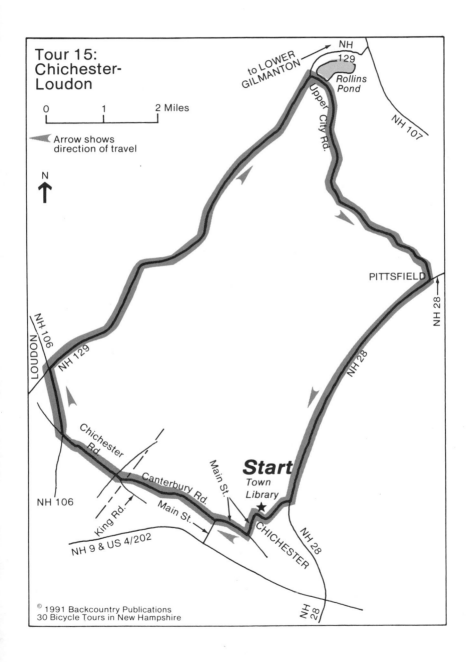

Tour 15:
Chichester-
Loudon

0   1   2 Miles

Arrow shows
direction of travel

N

to LOWER
GILMANTON

NH
129

Rollins
Pond

Upper City Rd.

NH 107

PITTSFIELD

NH 28

NH 28

NH 106

LOUDON

NH 129

Chichester Rd.

Canterbury Rd.

NH 106

King Rd.

Main St.

Main St.

Start
Town
Library
★

CHICHESTER

NH 28

NH 9 & US 4/202

NH 28

© 1991 Backcountry Publications
30 Bicycle Tours in New Hampshire

and golf course and can be found in Chichester off NH 28, about three miles north of NH 9/US 4/US 202 (435-8061, 435-7465). The Hitching Post is a Colonial homestead less remotely and more conveniently located on NH 9/US 4/US 202, 7.5 miles east of Concord, Exit 15E off I-93 (798-4951).

The ride starts at the Chichester Town Library on Main Street, opposite a pasture.

0.0   From the library bear right onto Main Street and ride 1.1 mile to Canterbury Road.

You pass a typical tiny northern New England town, with Grange hall, churches, meeting halls, a fire department, and a town hall housed in Colonial and Victorian buildings. The charm and beauty of Chichester Village are not accidental. The original 1727 charter of Chichester was the model for future charters in undivided parts of New Hampshire. These land grants, issued by the colony's pre-Revolutionary governors, required the settlers within three to five years to plant and cultivate the land and to build roads, dwelling houses, a school, and a church.

1.1   At the United Methodist Church, where Main Street makes a sharp left, stay on Canterbury Road, which continues straight for 2.1 miles toward a T-junction.

Canterbury Road is typical of backcountry New Hampshire lanes, with a less-than-smooth surface, adequate visibility, level-to-rolling terrain, open and shaded parts, and little traffic.

3.2   At the T-junction turn right on King Road, riding toward Loudon for 1.7 miles to NH 106.

Like many a New Hampshire road, King Road changes its name. In Loudon it becomes Chichester Road. This road is similar to Canterbury Road.

4.9   At the intersection with NH 106, turn right and ride for 0.9 mile to the intersection of NH 129.

NH 106, a major road, is well traveled, but it is level and smooth, with good visibility and an excellent lane-wide shoulder.

5.8   At the sign for Gilmanton at the Fox Pond Plaza shopping center, turn right on NH 129 East and ride 7.8 miles to Upper City Road in Gilmanton.

The Fox Pond Plaza has food and drink if you've forgotten to bring some.

You travel past pastures sprinkled with Holstein cows and an occasional Guernsey or Jersey, past corn fields and vegetable and fruit stands and an occasional sign inviting you to pick your own blueberries, raspberries, or strawberries, or to watch the making of apple cider or maple syrup, depending on the calendar.

NH 129 is a recently surfaced, silky smooth, double-yellow-line road with moderate visibility. It hugs the hills as they take you up and down over sometimes open, sometimes shaded terrain.

13.6 **Take a right on Upper City Road (unmarked) at Rollins Pond, preceded by a diamond black-on-yellow right-turn directional sign. The turn is past a stone wall on the right at a T-junction with NH 129, where a driveway descends toward the pond. The driveway is guarded by two granite posts, the left one inscribed "Pine Haven." Ride for 5.2 miles to NH 28.**

(Should you miss this turn, not to worry. In about 1 mile, NH 129 comes to a T-junction with NH 107. Go right on NH 107 for about 4 miles to NH 28. Go right again and ride about 5 miles, which will land you at the 23.1-mile direction below.)

You have a steep climb for about 0.5 mile on Upper City Road, which is shaded mercifully by an elegant colonnade of maple trees and the few surviving elm trees in the region. This is the most rural part of the ride, taking you to ridges and elevations offering spectacular panoramas of the countryside, past farms and orchards and graceful Colonial houses.

Especially attractive is Montavista or Mountainview Orchard, at the top of the hill, 17 miles into the ride. The orchard is centered on a large white double-chimney Colonial house by a stone wall adjacent to a barn with a cupola, atop which is perched a golden eagle weathervane. The orchard offers peaches in early August and early apples later in the month.

Upper City Road is typically rural New Hampshire, with frost heaves, twists and turns, and even about 0.2 mile of packed-dirt surface once you have completed the climb from NH 129. On the ridges, the road tends to be smoother and more open with very little traffic. Be cautious, however, after the Mountainview Orchard, when the road plunges around a sharp left curve.

18.4 **At the junction turn right onto NH 28 South and ride 4.7 miles to Main Street in Chichester.**

On this stretch at about 2 miles you pass the Fox Glove Restaurant on the left. Across the road from it is the Crack of Dawn Restaurant and Bakery. Frekey's Dairy Freeze, next to the justice of the peace's house, will be about a half-mile on the right before your next turn.

Like NH 106, NH 28 is a major road with steady traffic, but it is generally flat and smooth, with good visibility and a lane-wide shoulder.

23.1 **Merge right, away from NH 28 and onto Main Street at the Chichester Country Store and ride 1.0 mile to the Chichester library.**

The store, established in 1847, is a favorite Saturday-morning stop of the Granite State Wheelmen. Inside, it serves daily special sandwiches, while outside it displays a bulletin board for the community of 1,900 people.

The last mile is up a steep grade, known sometimes locally as "Mount deSpagna."

24.1 **You're back where you started.**

Bicycle Repair Services
Cycle Fix (bicycle road service) (269-3608)
Haggett's Bicycle Shop, 77 South Main Street, Concord (9–5:30 Mon.–Thur., Sat.; 9–9 Fri.) (228-0565)
S&W Sport Shop, 238 South Main Street, Concord (9–6 Mon.–Thur.; 9–8 Fri.; 9–6 Sat.) (228-1441)
Waite Sports Specialists, 12 North Main Street, Concord (9–6 Mon.–Thur.; 9–8 Fri.; 9–5:30 Sat.) (228-8621)

16
Concord-Hopkinton

14.2 miles; easy cycling
Level to rolling terrain, with several short hills

Offering an excellent introduction to cycle touring, the Concord-Hopkinton tour couples easy biking along little-traveled roads with convenient access to New Hampshire's capital. Although about half the tour is within Concord city limits, the roads take you past several ponds and farms as well as the grounds of St. Paul's School. Covering just a bit more than 14 miles, the tour is ideal for a morning or afternoon jaunt and is suited particularly for introducing the family to bicycle touring. However, you may want to try another tour in this book on Labor Day weekend, when the Hopkinton Fair generates very busy traffic. For information on accommodations in the area, consult Tours 9 and 18.

Start adjacent to Exit 3 (Stickney Hill Road) of I-89, about 4 miles northwest of the intersection of I-89 and I-93 south of Concord. A short access road on the south side of I-89 leads off Stickney Hill Road to a bicycle path. Park alongside this access road at the bike path and begin your trip.

0.0   **Start up Stickney Hill Road, a smoothly surfaced way rising sharply for about 0.3 mile, and ride 1.4 miles to Farrington Corner Road.**

1.4   **Turn right at Farrington Corner Road and ride 2.1 miles to Jewett Road.**

Farrington Corner Road is narrow, bumpy, and nearly free of traffic. Much of it is shaded by an arcade of tree branches, rising gradually to Jewett Road, passing attractive farms and homes.

3.5   **Turn right on Jewett Road (unmarked) and ride 0.6 mile over the Interstate to US 202/NH 9/NH 103.**

At the junction Boulder Farm produces acres of strawberries. In June or early July you can "pick your own" and treat yourself to a feast.

4.1   **At the T-junction of US 202/NH 9/NH 103 and Jewett Road, turn left and ride 1.1 miles through the center of Hopkinton to the**

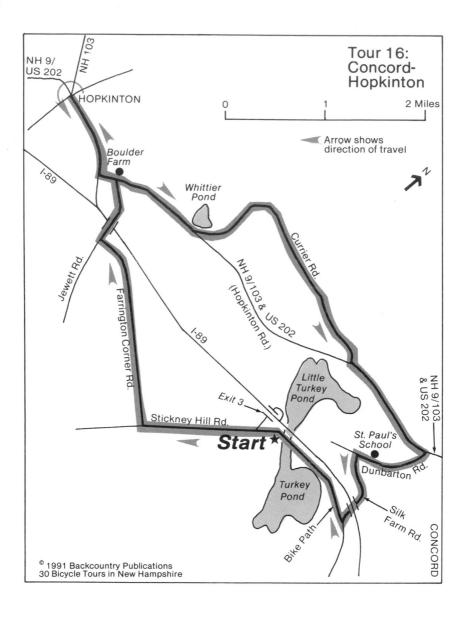

Tour 16:
Concord-
Hopkinton

0   1   2 Miles

◀ Arrow shows
direction of travel

N

NH 9/
US 202

NH 103

HOPKINTON

Boulder
Farm

Whittier
Pond

Currier Rd.

I-89

Jewett Rd.

Farrington Corner Rd.

NH 9/103 & US 202
(Hopkinton Rd.)

I-89

Exit 3

Stickney Hill Rd.

Start ★

Little
Turkey
Pond

NH 9/103 & US 202

St. Paul's
School

Dunbarton Rd.

Turkey
Pond

Bike Path

Silk
Farm Rd.

CONCORD

© 1991 Backcountry Publications
30 Bicycle Tours in New Hampshire

general store, the Cracker Barrel. Here NH 103 diverges to the right from US 202/NH 9 toward Contoocook.

Hopkinton's main street is worth a visit for the beautiful Colonials, large white churches, and town hall, set back from the road lined with magnificent shade trees. On the village green, St. Andrew's Church was designed by John Leach and built in 1827. It is of Granite Ashlar construction, a style typical of New England Episcopal churches of the period.

The Cracker Barrel is a well-stocked country store (7–7 Mon.–Fri., 8–7 Sat., 8–4 Sun.). The Horseshoe Tavern on US 202/NH 9/NH 103, a half-mile west of Jewett Road (5–9 Tues.–Fri., till 10 Sat.–Sun. for dinner; 11:30–2 Tues.–Fri. for lunch; 11–2 Sun. for brunch, 746-4501) offers elegant country dining overlooking Smith Pond. Reservations are preferred.

US 202/NH 9/NH 103 is a wide two-lane road with no shoulder. Since it is near an I-89 interchange, this section of road tends to have more traffic than other parts of the route, but road visibility is good and the speed limit is slow. The terrain is generally flat.

5.2   From The Cracker Barrel, retrace your route 1.1 miles to the junction of Jewett Road. Continue east on US 202/NH 9/NH 103 an additional mile to Currier Road (unmarked) on the left. Note Whittier Pond on your left just before the turn.

Here US 202/NH 9/NH 103 (Hopkinton Road) is wide with no shoulder but a new surface with light-to-moderate traffic, descending as you leave Hopkinton.

7.3   By Whittier Pond, turn left and follow the unmarked Currier Road for 2.7 miles until it rejoins US 202/NH 9/NH 103 (Hopkinton Road).

Narrow, with a good surface, no shoulder, and well shaded, Currier Road offers a gentle downhill from the rush of traffic and a grand view of a New England farm on your left.

10.0   At the junction with US 202/NH 9/NH 103, turn left and ride 1.2 miles to Dunbarton Road.

The numbered road remains wide with no shoulder and moderate traffic, allowing you to coast most of the first mile, with a short steep uphill just before your next turn.

11.2   Turn right onto Dunbarton Road, with Millville School on your left, at the "St. Paul's School" sign, and ride 0.8 mile to Silk Farm Road on your left.

St. Paul's School, a private, coeducational boarding school on 1,800 acres of woods and open land, with manicured grounds and Gothic-style buildings, invites you for a rest.

Dunbarton Road is smooth and nearly level, with no shoulder and almost no traffic.

12.0 **At Silk Farm Road, turn left and ride another 0.8 mile, passing under I-89, where the bicycle path leads off sharply to the right.** For a swimming detour, rather than turning left at Silk Farm Road, continue straight past the car-barrier gate to the docks of St. Paul's School, which despite the oxymoronic "No Trespassing Without

Bicycling in the Concord-Hopkinton area is a year-round activity.

Courtesy Frec McLaughlin/Haggett's Bike Shop, Concord

Permission" sign at Silk Farm Road, graciously offers cyclists Turkey Pond's inviting waters, a favorite "secret" swimming spot of the Granite State Wheelmen.

Silk Farm Road is flat and shaded.

12.8 **Immediately beyond the I-89 underpass, make a hairpin right turn onto the paved bicycle path. It parallels the interstate for 1.4 miles and leads you back to the starting point.**

The 8-foot bicycle path is smooth, but look out for speed bumps, runners, bicycles, and occasional stray motorcycles and mopeds.

14.2 **You are back at your car at the other end of the bicycle path.**

Audubon House (9–5 Mon.–Fri., 9–3 Sun.) on Silk Farm Road 0.2 mile beyond the entrance to the bicycle path is the headquarters of the Audubon Society of New Hampshire. It features a gift shop, library, and several walking paths.

Bicycle Repair Services

Haggett's Bicycle Shop, 77 South Main Street, Concord (9–5:30 Mon.–Thur., Sat., 9–9 Fri.) (228-0565)

S&W Sport Shop, 238 South Main Street, Concord (9–6 Mon.–Thur.; 9–8 Fri.; 9–3 Sat.) (228-1441)

Waite Sports Specialists, 12 North Main Street, Concord (9–6 Mon.–Thur.; 9–8 Fri.; 9–5:30 Sat.) (228-8621)

17
Dunbarton-Goffstown

23 miles
Moderately challenging

Situated between the cities of Concord and Manchester, the Dunbarton-Goffstown tour offers southern New Hampshire and Boston-area cyclists quick, easy access to the rural beauty and backroad touring of the Granite State. It is pleasantly surprising how quickly the urban environment of Manchester, New England's largest city north of Boston, gives way to the small towns, hamlets, and country living that predominate on this tour. Set up in a figure eight, this tour is relatively short, and we have purposely kept it that way because it is hilly. Pains were taken to plan the route with a lot of descents to offset the hill climbs. Anyone even moderately fit should experience no serious difficulty with it. However, a good granny gear would serve well and help flatten out the upward pulls, most of which are gradual.

And there are rewards for your efforts! Besides enjoying some long descents, you will see sweeping views of southern New Hampshire along NH 13. Clough State Park has swimming and picnicking in the summer months. Dunbarton offers a glimpse of traditional New England architecture with its town hall, Congregational Church, and white frame buildings. Finally, Goffstown, with its old Victorian and Colonial homes and several good eating places, is a spot to enjoy a break midway through the tour. If you have time visit Concord, a tour of the state-of-the-art Christa McAuliffe Planetarium (271-2842) is a must (Exit 14, I-93).

The tour begins at Dunbarton Country Store at the junction of NH 13 and Winslow Road in Dunbarton. To get there, follow NH 13 for 5 miles south from the I-89 overpass in Concord, or take NH 13 north for 8.6 miles from its junction with NH 114 in Goffstown. Park along Winslow Road. Dunbarton Country Store (7–8 Mon.–Sat., 8–7 Sun.), in addition to groceries, has a deli with a good assortment of fresh sandwiches.

0.0 Start by following Winslow Road/Stark Lane for 1.5 miles to its junction with Mansion Road.

Winslow Road is a shoulderless two-lane road that rises and dips frequently. Note the fork after 0.8 mile: bear left at this junction, which becomes Stark Lane (unmarked).

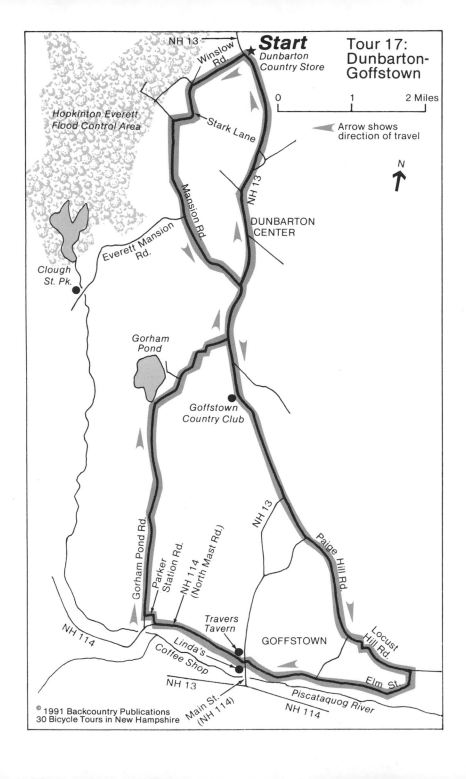

NH 13

Winslow Rd.

Start
Dunbarton Country Store

Tour 17:
Dunbarton-
Goffstown

Hopkinton Everett
Flood Control Area

Stark Lane

0   1   2 Miles

Arrow shows
direction of travel

N

NH 13

DUNBARTON
CENTER

Mansion Rd.

Everett Mansion
Rd.

Clough
St. Pk.

Gorham
Pond

Goffstown
Country Club

NH 13

Paige Hill Rd.

Gorham Pond Rd.

Parker
Station Rd.

NH 114
(North Mast Rd.)

Travers
Tavern

Locust
Hill Rd.

NH 114

Linda's
Coffee Shop

GOFFSTOWN

Elm St.

NH 13

Main St.
(NH 114)

Piscataquog River

NH 114

© 1991 Backcountry Publications
30 Bicycle Tours in New Hampshire

After immediately going past a bog, the road passes through a heavily wooded section including Dunbarton Town Forest.

1.5 Turn left on Mansion Road and ride 2.6 miles to the junction with NH 13.

Mansion Road is a two-lane road of the same quality as Winslow Road and Stark Lane. It rises gradually most of the way to NH 13, then ascends rather steeply for 0.7 mile just before joining NH 13.

At 2.8 miles you come to the junction of Mansion Road and Everett Mansion Road with clearly marked signs to Clough State Park and Everett Dam. Should you wish to picnic and swim at Clough State Park or take a look at Everett Dam, which is part of the Hopkinton-Everett Flood Control Area, turn right on Everett Mansion Road and ride 1.25 miles.

4.1 Turn right and proceed for 3 miles to unmarked Paige Hill Road, on the left side of NH 13 in the middle of a sharp righthand curve.

NH 13, wider than Mansion Road with a smooth surface and light-to-moderate traffic, ascends gradually for 1.8 miles to Goffstown Country Club, the highest point on the trip, then descends for 0.8 mile. There are beautiful views to the south and west on this section.

Goffstown Country Club (774-5031) is open to the public and has a snack bar open during daylight hours overlooking the beautiful ninth fairway.

7.1 Turn left onto Paige Hill Road (unmarked) 0.4 mile after the Goffstown line, and follow it for 2.2 miles to a fork. Take the left fork, Locust Hill Road, and ride 1 mile to its junction with Elm Street.

Paige Hill Road is a narrow two-lane road with no shoulder and surfaces varying from smooth to frost heaves. It is quite ridable and traffic is normally very light. With the exception of a slight rise of 0.2 mile, this section descends gradually, then steeply, so enjoy!

Round Wheel Orchard, where you can buy fruit in season, is located on the left at 8.2 miles.

10.3 Turn right on Elm Street and ride 2.6 miles to the junction of Elm Street with NH 114 and NH 13.

Elm Street is about as wide and smooth as NH 13 and carries moderate traffic because it connects Goffstown with Manchester. With the exception of a short ascent of 0.2 mile as soon as you turn onto Elm Street, the road stays mostly level as it approaches Goffstown along the banks of the Piscataquog River.

At 11.1 miles a sandy beach invites with a sign: "Swim at your own risk as per order of selectmen."

Travers Tavern (dinner 5:30–10 Tues.–Sat., call 497-3978 for reservations) is a very nice restaurant located on NH 13 just a few hundred feet from the junction of Elm Street, NH 114, and NH 13. Serving a Continental menu, it caters more to the leisurely diner than to sweaty cyclists clad in bike shorts and T-shirts. But it offers a nice end to a day of cycling when you can arrive in more suitable clothing.

Linda's Coffee Shop and Bakery (5–6 Mon.–Thurs., 5–8 Fri. and Sat., 5–3 Sun., 497-2222) is better suited to a weary cyclist with a big appetite and an insatiable sweet tooth. Located on the Main Street (NH 114) of Goffstown just a few yards to the left of the junction of Elm Street and NH 114, it features inexpensive daily specials.

12.9 **Turn right followed by an immediate left onto NH 114 North (North Mast Road) and ride 1.3 miles to Parker Station Road. Turn right, ride 0.1 mile to Gorham Pond Road. Turn right again and ride 4.3 miles to the junction of NH 13.**

NH 114 is a two-lane road with moderate traffic. After 0.6 mile the shoulder is paved. Nice old Colonials and Victorian homes grace this section of town.

Gorham Pond Road is a narrow two-lane road through pleasant country. It rises gradually all the way to NH 114.

The Goffstown Historical Society is at the corner of Parker Station Road and Gorham Pond Road.

18.9 **Turn left on NH 13 and ride 4.1 miles back to Dunbarton.**

From Gorham Pond Road to Mansion Road, a distance of 0.7 mile, you duplicate a section of NH 13 ridden earlier in the ride.

At 20.3 miles you are in the village of Dunbarton, with its traditional New England architecture.

At 21.3 miles begin a steep 1.7-mile descent to end your day.

23.0 **Your tour ends at Dunbarton Country Store.**

Bicycle Repair Services
The Bike Barn, 255 Maple Street, Manchester (9–5 Mon.–Fri.; 9–4 Sat.) (668-6555)
Bike Doctor, 225 Laurel Street, Manchester (9:30–7:30 Mon.–Fri.; 9:30–5 Sat.) (627-5566)
Haggett's Bicycle Shop, 920 Second Street, Manchester (9–6 Mon.–Fri.; 9–5 Sat.; closed Tue. and Sun.) (624-8362)
Haggett's Bicycle Shop, 77 South Main Street, Concord (9–5:30 Mon.–Sat.; 9–9 Fri.) (228-0565)
Jake's Bicycle Shop, 414 Kelley Street, Manchester (9–6 Mon.–Wed., Fri.; 9–8 Thur.; 9–3 Sat.) (669-5422)

Nault's, 30-32 Bridge Street, Manchester (9–6 Mon.–Wed.; 9–8 Thur.–Fri.; 9–5 Sat.) (669-7993)

S&W Sport Shop, 238 South Main Street., Concord (9–6 Mon.–Thur.; 9–8 Fri.; 9–3:30 Sat.) (228-1441)

Ultrasports of New England, 832 Elm Street, Manchester (9–8 Mon., Thur., Fri.; 9–6 Tue., Wed., Sat.) (668-6347)

Waite Sports Specialists, 12 North Main Street, Concord (9–6 Mon.–Thur.; 9–8 Fri.; 9–5:30 Sat.) (228-8621)

18

Shaker Village—McAuliffe Planetarium

25.3 miles; moderate cycling
Several short, steep hills

This ride joins current and historical textures of New Hampshire life: the super high-tech Christa McAuliffe Planetarium, and the religious community of the Shakers.

In 1792, a celibate religious sect from Manchester, England, known as the Shakers, established a settlement of converts on the farm of Benjamin Whitcher in Canterbury, New Hampshire. At its height in 1850, the community consisted of 250 faithful operating a commercial agricultural system of 6,000 acres, with 100 buildings, including dwellings, workshops, barns, and water-powered mills. Remaining are 22 structures that demonstrate the architecture and house the furniture and crafts of these gifted people. Guided tours, a gift shop, and a restaurant serving traditional Shaker food are offered. This village is similar to the Shaker community-museum that you can enjoy on the Potter Place-Lake Mascoma tour (Tour 13).

Concord is the home of the Christa McAuliffe Planetarium, a state-of-the art planetarium that stands as a memorial to the Concord schoolteacher who perished in the 1986 explosion of the *Challenger* space shuttle.

Offering moderate terrain, light traffic, and refreshing views of the Merrimack Valley Region, this trip particularly appeals to families with young aspiring cyclists and to history buffs who need an intellectual excuse for a bike ride.

You may wish to avoid this tour during the third weekend in June, when thousands of motorcyclists descend on the New Hampshire International Speedway on NH 106 for the Loudon Classic Motorcycle Races, the oldest races of their kind in the United States. But if you ride this route on the fourth Saturday in July, you will be delighted with the Canterbury Fair, a tiny, homey festival of arts, crafts, books, games, antiques, Morris dancers, children's animals, and the world's best lemonade, on the village green.

For those wishing to make a weekend of it, Concord is a pleasant city with a small-town atmosphere. While there are no country inns within its environs, several motels provide suitable accommodations, including the Brick Tower (224-9565), Concord Coach (224-2511), and the Ramada Inn (224-9534). Eagle Square, a recently renovated downtown mini-mall, has many boutiques, shops, and restaurants. Bicentennial Plaza, completed in 1987, added more of the same. On the eastern outskirts at the junction of US 4/US 202/NH 9/NH 106/I-393 is the Steeplegate Mall, opened in the summer of 1990.

Among the downtown restaurants are Hermano's and Tio Juan's (Mexican), Thursday's (crepes, quiches, breads, soups), B. Mae Denny's (informal in-town dining), Foodee's (for the best pizza in New Hampshire), and Vercelli's (Italian).

The tour starts in the parking lot of the Christa McAuliffe Planetarium. To get there, follow I-93 to I-393 (at Exit 15E). Take the first exit off I-393, marked Fort Eddy Road/New Hampshire Technical Institute (NHTI). At the T-junction at the end of the exit ramp, turn left and follow the signs to the planetarium.

0.0 **From the planetarium, turn left and ride about 30 yards to a bike path that begins on the right just before the bridge over I-93. Proceed with ultimate caution and discretion along this very narrow path, the only crossing of the Merrimack River convenient to this ride. Ride the bike path for 0.6 mile to its junction with Eastman Street in East Concord. Follow Eastman Street for 0.4 mile to its junction with NH 132, East Side Drive.**

Food is available at the Mill Stream Market on Eastman Street.

Note the historical monument on Eastman Road commemorating Captain Ebenezer Eastman, first settler of Concord in 1727, who established the first ferry in the same year on this site.

1.0 **Bear left on NH 132 North (Mountain Road) and ride for 6.6 miles to an unmarked road on the right noted by a sign directing you to Canterbury Center and Shaker Village.**

Bridges House, the official governor's residence, is on the left side of NH 132, 0.2 mile north of the Eastman Street intersection. This brick Colonial was built in 1836 and donated to the state by Styles Bridges, former governor of New Hampshire and U.S. senator.

NH 132 is a two-lane road with a smooth surface, no shoulder, and generally low traffic. It has several short steep hills, especially near Concord Country Club at 2.2 miles, but usually it rolls moderately.

Open westerly views of the Merrimack Valley can be seen at 2.4 miles just beyond Blye Farm Condominiums.

7.6 **At the intersection of NH 132 and the road to Canterbury Center, turn right and proceed 1.2 miles to the junction of Baptist Road in**

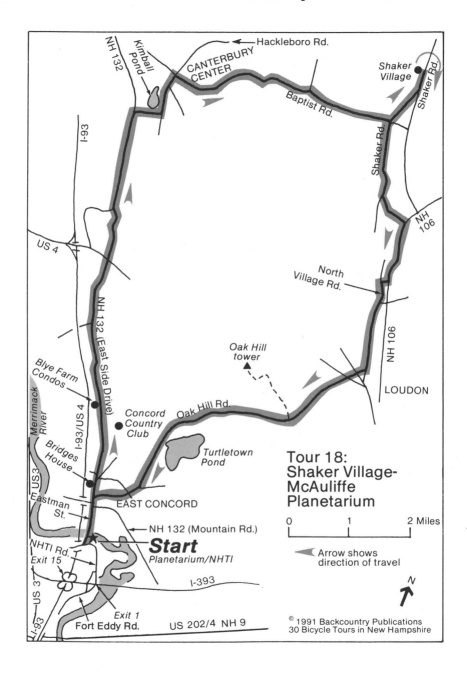

Hackleboro Rd.

NH 132

Kimball Pond

CANTERBURY CENTER

Shaker Village

Shaker Rd.

Baptist Rd.

I-93

Shaker Rd.

NH 106

US 4

North Village Rd.

NH 132 (East Side Drive)

NH 106

Oak Hill tower

LOUDON

Blye Farm Condos

Merrimack River

I-93/US 4

Concord Country Club

Oak Hill Rd.

Bridges House

US 3

Turtletown Pond

**Tour 18:
Shaker Village-
McAuliffe
Planetarium**

Eastman St.

EAST CONCORD

0   1   2 Miles

NHTI Rd.

Exit 15

NH 132 (Mountain Rd.)

Start
Planetarium/NHTI

◄ Arrow shows
direction of travel

US 3

I-93

I-393

N

Exit 1
Fort Eddy Rd.   US 202/4 NH 9

© 1991 Backcountry Publications
30 Bicycle Tours in New Hampshire

Canterbury Center. Note that there is a T-intersection after 0.4 mile. Bear left and continue to Canterbury Center.

Kimball Pond Conservation Area is on the left after 0.5 mile.

The road surface is not as smooth as NH 132, but it is very ridable. There is no shoulder, but traffic is light. A steep hill, 0.2 mile long, is located just beyond Kimball Pond.

8.8 Following signs for Shaker Village and Loudon, turn right on Baptist Road (unmarked) opposite Hackleboro Road, and ride 3.9 miles to its junction with Shaker Road (unmarked).

The picturesque village of Canterbury Center has a town hall, church, library, and general store, which offers an opportunity for a rest stop or snack.

Baptist Road has some short, steep ascents and descents. The road's surface, although adequate for riding, has frost heaves. The area is wooded with occasional bogs. You also will see several nicely restored houses.

Courtesy Christa McAuliffe Planetarium

The Shaker Village tour begins at the planetarium in Concord.

12.7 **Turn left on Shaker Road and ride 1 mile to Shaker Village.**
Shaker Village is open Tuesday through Saturday and holiday Mondays, from mid-May through Mid-October, 10–5. Knowledgeable guides, who interpret 200 years of Shaker history, lead hour-long walking tours of six historical buildings. Craftsmen offer demonstrations in Shaker basketmaking, tinsmithing, woodworking, and sewing.

The Creamery (10–4:30, lunch 11:30–3), a building where cream and butter were once made, serves traditional Shaker meals at moderate prices, from $1.95 to $5.95. There is also a picnic area for those who choose to bring a lunch.

13.7 **After a visit to Shaker Village retrace your route south on Shaker Road for 1 mile, then continue straight ahead for another 1.7 miles to the junction of NH 106 in Loudon.**
The Beanstalk General Store and a small shopping center are at the junction of Shaker Road and NH 106.

16.4 **Turn right and head south on NH 106 for exactly 1 mile to North Village Road.**
NH 106 is a two-lane road with a wide, paved shoulder, smooth surface, and moderate traffic.

17.4 **Turn right on North Village Road, which makes an immediate sharp left, and follow it through a residential and commercial area for 1.6 miles to Oak Hill Road on the right.**

19.0 **Turn right on Oak Hill Road (unmarked), follow it straight through two intersections, and continue for 5.2 miles to its junction with NH 132, Mountain Road. Note that Oak Hill Road changes to Shawmut Road at its junction with NH 132.**
Oak Hill Road is a two-lane shoulderless road with light traffic. It offers a fair surface that improves when you cross into Concord. It climbs 0.6 mile then descends all the way to NH 132.

Loudon Village Antiques is on Oak Hill Road 0.1 mile beyond its junction with North Village Road. According to the proprietor, a retired gentleman who lives there, it is open "most of the time" or by appointment (783-4741).

At the top of the 0.6-mile climb, excellent views of Concord and Turtletown Pond are to your left. For the ambitious there is a 2-mile walk to the Oak Hill Lookout Tower.

As you descend toward Concord you pass several beautiful country houses as well as Turtletown Pond Conservation Area.

24.3 **Turn left on NH 132, past the Exxon Station, take an immediate right on Eastman Street, and retrace your route for 1 mile.**

Photo by Judy Northrup-Bennett/Canterbury Shaker Village

Canterbury Shaker Village, one of New Hampshire's two Shaker Museums (both visited by tours in this book).

25.3   Return to your starting point, the Christa McAuliffe Planetarium (271-2842), to which a visit is a must!

Bicycle Repair Services

Cycle Fix (bicycle road service) (569–8292)

Haggett's Bicycle Shop, 77 South Main Street, Concord (9–5:30 Mon.–Sat.; 9–9 Fri.) (228-0565)

S&W Sport Shop, 238 South Main Street., Concord (9–6 Mon.–Thur.; 9–8 Fri.; 9–3:30 Sat.) (228-1441)

Waite Sports Specialists, 12 North Main Street, Concord (9–6 Mon.–Thur.; 9–8 Fri.; 9–5:30 Sat.) (228-8621)

Southeastern
New Hampshire

19
Nottingham-Epping

27.0 miles; easy to moderate cycling
Rolling terrain, several hills

Although Rockingham County is one of the nation's fastest-growing regions, don't let that deter your from exploring its off-the-main-road expanses—yours to enjoy just an interstate exit or two north of the Boston area. Even as metropolitan Massachusetts overflows northward into New Hampshire, this area nonetheless manages to maintain its rural character and charisma along shaded two-lane roads, and its feeling of village rather than suburb. Once on this route, there's hardly a hint that you're just 50 miles north of the hub of New England.

As you ride past dairy farms and orchards, you pass through neighborhoods where the old and new coexist. Colonials adjacent to condominiums, country stores adjacent to fast-food outlets. North of hectic NH 101, this rectangular ride begins at its northwestern corner in Pawtuckaway State Park and defines an area bounded by Nottingham, Lee in neighboring Strafford County, Epping, and Raymond. It takes you along rolling hills with smooth surfaces and lighter-than-normal traffic through one of New Hampshire's earliest-settled regions. Much of the ride follows the North and Lamprey rivers, where you discover remnants of nineteenth-century mills and Colonial forests that raised "tall pine trees" for the masts of the Royal Navy. Nottingham is where Colonel Henry Dearborn trained his militia before marching to the Battle of Lexington, while Raymond is named after Captain William Raymond of Massachusetts, who raised a company of soldiers to fight in Quebec. Pawtuckaway, a premier New Hampshire state park, offers recreation, from camping to fishing, from hiking to swimming. And if you bring your mountain bike, you can sample the miles of the park's glorious trails. The park is off Exit 5 of NH 101, easily accessible from I-93 to the west and I-95 to the east. The area is about midway between the Seacoast and Merrimack Valley regions. If you make this an overnight jaunt, for lodging other than first-come, first-served, first-class camping at the park (895-3031), see Tours 16, 17, and 18.

Start from the park's Visitors Center and Camping Registration parking lot.

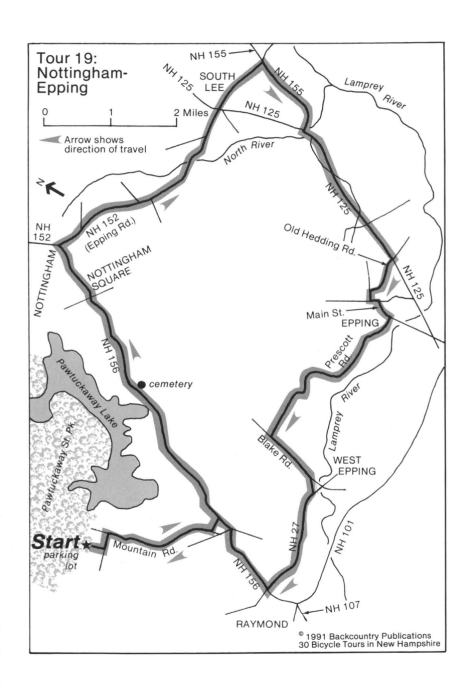

Tour 19:
Nottingham-
Epping

0   1   2 Miles

Arrow shows
direction of travel

N

NH 155

SOUTH
LEE

NH 125

NH 155

Lamprey River

NH 125

North River

NH 125

NH 152

NH 152
(Epping Rd.)

NOTTINGHAM

NOTTINGHAM
SQUARE

Old Hedding Rd.

NH 125

Main St.

EPPING

Prescott Rd

NH 156

Pawtuckaway Lake

cemetery

Pawtuckaway St. Pk.

Lamprey River

Blake Rd.

WEST
EPPING

Start ★

parking
lot

Mountain Rd.

NH 27

NH 101

NH 156

NH 107

RAYMOND

© 1991 Backcountry Publications
30 Bicycle Tours in New Hampshire

0.0 **From the parking lot, turn left and ride 0.1 mile to the stop sign on Mountain Road.**

0.1 **Turn right onto Mountain Road and ride 2 miles to a T-junction with NH 156.**

At 0.9 mile on the right at the Mountain Road Post, you can rent a canoe or a bicycle. At 1.4 miles on the left the Kindred Place store (open summers only) offers food and drink.

The park is on top of a mountain and thus Mountain Road is hilly, but mostly a downgrade with a good surface, no shoulder, and little traffic.

2.1 **At the T-junction with NH 156 where a sign directs you right toward Raymond and left toward Northwood, turn left on NH 156 North and ride 5.2 miles to NH 152 (Epping Road) in Nottingham.**

At 4.6 miles on the right is a tiny picture-postcard cemetery along a mostly shaded route that opens occasionally on farmland vistas. At 6.3 miles you pass through Nottingham Square, then immediately soar downhill for one mile, past the Congregational Church at 6.7 miles, to a stop sign and NH 152.

NH 156 has a smooth surface, with less-than-perfect shoulders but only moderate traffic along rolling terrain. Its near-perfect downhills allow you to gather enough speed to slingshot over the upgrades.

7.3 **At the stop sign opposite a brown house, make a hairpin right turn onto NH 152 East (Epping Road) and ride 4.7 miles to NH 155.**

At 7.2 miles you pass Liar's Paradise store and gas station, where the community's stalwarts gather to tell tall tales around the proverbial pickle barrel and potbellied stove. At 9.9 miles the road turns sharply right as it crosses a bridge over the North River and enters Lee. To the right immediately after the bridge is Harvey's Mill, an abandoned ancient wooden structure perched above the river, a delightful rest or lunch stop from which you can admire an early-eighteenth-century red-brick Colonial house with an elegant sunburst over the front door. At 10.9 miles you cross NH 125 in South Lee.

NH 152 is similar to NH 156. The surface becomes silky-smooth and the grade levels out once you cross NH 125, essentially more downhill than not.

12.0 **At the intersection with NH 155 at a white four-chimney Federal house to your left, turn right toward Epping, and ride 1.4 miles.**

NH 155 is similar to NH 152.

13.4 **Turn left onto NH 125 South and ride 2.5 miles to Old Hedding Road.**

Farms and orchards greet you and slide away as you wend your way south, past the intersection of NH 87 at 15 miles, the Rose Country Variety store at 15.7 miles, and the Road Runner restaurant that advertises Italian food and subs at 15.9 miles.

NH 125 is smooth and generally level, with busier traffic, but a lanewide shoulder as well.

15.9 **Just yards after the Road Runner restaurant and feet before a "Division of Motor Vehicles—State Police" sign, turn right onto Old Hedding Road and ride 0.8 mile.**

16.7 **Turn left at the stop sign by a horse farm, where the road becomes Main Street, and ride 0.1 mile.**

16.8 **Bear right for 0.3 mile along Main Street at downtown Epping.**

17.1 **Turn right onto Prescott Road, past a cemetery on your left, and ride 2.9 miles to a T-junction with Blake Road (unmarked).**

You ride past orchards and Colonial houses, with the Governor

Lunching on the Nottingham-Epping tour.

Prescott House at 18.6 miles demanding your admiration.

With the exception of about 0.2 mile of rough surface and some typical backcountry New Hampshire frost heaves, most of Prescott Road is a recently paved silky-smooth roller-coaster of a shady lane whose soaring downs give you momentum to make it over most of the ups quite easily.

20.0 **Turn left at the T-junction of Blake Road (unmarked) and ride 1.2 miles to NH 27.**

Blake Road has equal lengths of recently paved rolling surfaces and rougher frost-heave stretches.

21.2 **At the stop sign directly opposite the West Epping Village Market, turn right on NH 27 West and ride 2.3 miles to the intersection of NH 107/NH 27/NH 101 Business/NH 156.**

NH 27 is a wide, recently paved two-lane road, flat to rolling, with a short stretch of rough 1930s concrete surface in Raymond and a sufficient shoulder.

23.5 **In the junction, seek out NH 156, turn right, and ride 1.4 miles to Mountain Road.**

As NH 156 rises uphill on a smooth surface, the shoulder narrows.

24.9 **Turn left onto Mountain Road and ride 2 miles to the Pawtuckaway Park entrance road on your left.**

26.9 **Turn left at the Pawtuckaway Park entrance and ride 0.1 mile to the Visitors Center and Camping Registration parking lot on your right.**

27.0 **You're back where you began your ride.**

Bicycle Repair Services

Durham Bike, Pette Brook Lane, Durham (9–6 Mon.–Fri.; 10–3 Sat.) (368-5634)

Exeter Cycles Bike Shop, 32 Portsmouth Avenue, Exeter (9:30–5:30 Mon.–Thur.; 9:30–7 Fri.; 9–5 Sat.) (778-2331).

Kingston Enterprises, 85 North Danville Road, off NH 125, Kingston, (9–5 Tue.–Sat.) (642-3506)

Transition Performance Racing, 75 Harriman Hill Road, Raymond (9–5 Mon.–Sat.) (895-6594)

Wheel Power, 37 Water Street, Exeter (9:30–5:30 Mon.–Sat) (772-6343)

20

New Hampshire-Maine: A Neighborly Tour

30.0 miles; easy cycling
Gently rolling terrain

Starting at the University of New Hampshire campus at Durham, this route loops through the oldest settlements in the state (1623) and takes you briefly into neighboring Maine, sampling the academic, agricultural, historic, and urban textures of the area. Geographically, New Hampshire is vital to Maine. Without its western neighbor, Maine would not be a part of the continental United States, because Maine is the only state among the lower 48 that borders on only one other state. The ride slides along the easiest 30 miles in New Hampshire, touching South Berwick, Maine, site of the region's earliest mills, the Berwick Academy boarding school, and birth and burial place of a nineteenth-century writer and chronicler of Maine and its people, Sarah Orne Jewett.

Stop and smell the flowers when you cycle by the Madbury Rose Farm and its 3,700 feet of greenhouses — among the world's longest. For a nominal one dollar, Elliott Rose Company employees will guide you on a tour of the blooming enterprise, which has been flourishing since 1901, producing up to a half-million roses annually. If vegetables and fruits are more to your taste, visit Tuttle's Red Barn on Dover Point, the outlet for America's oldest family farm, granted to barrelmaker John Tuttle in 1632 by King Charles I — a national agricultural landmark on the Great Bay saltwater estuary. Additional agricultural distractions abound about 20 miles north on NH 16 in Milton at the New Hampshire Farm Museum, among whose artifacts is the three-holer outhouse from the homestead of Horace "Go West Young Man" Greeley, one of many famous New Hampshire sons.

The University of New Hampshire campus at Durham, with its 12,000 students, offers diversions and entertainment from art galleries and athletics to music and drama. Dover, one of New Hampshire's oldest English settlements and an early inland commercial center of the Seacoast, is a compact city with the customary offerings of dining and nightlife, rivaled only by its neighbor Portsmouth. For a special celebration, Yankee Sunrise offers weekend champagne flights aboard hot-air

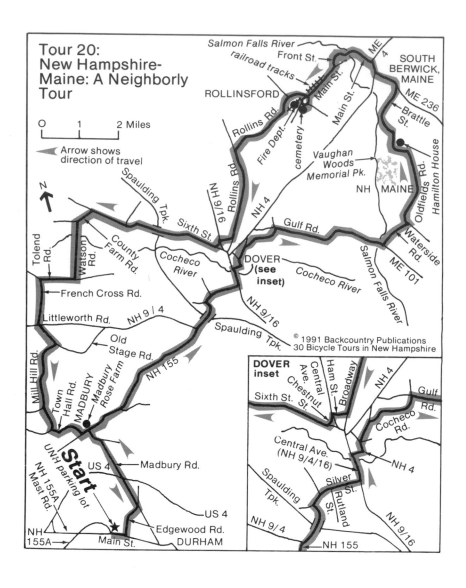

Tour 20:
New Hampshire-
Maine: A Neighborly
Tour

O   1   2 Miles

◀ Arrow shows
direction of travel

N

Salmon Falls River

Front St.

railroad tracks

ROLLINSFORD

SOUTH
BERWICK,
MAINE

ME

4

ME 236

Brattle
St.

Main St.

Main St.

Rollins Rd.

Fire Dept.

cemetery

Vaughan
Woods
Memorial Pk.

Hamilton House

Oldfields Rd.

NH   MAINE

NH 9/16

Rollins Rd.

NH 4

Gulf Rd.

Waterside
Rd.

ME 101

Salmon Falls River

Spaulding Tpk.

Sixth St.

DOVER
(see
inset)

Cocheco River

Tolend
Rd.

Watson
Rd.

County
Farm Rd.

Cocheco
River

French Cross Rd.

Littleworth Rd.

NH 9 / 4

NH 9/16

Spaulding Tpk.

© 1991 Backcountry Publications
30 Bicycle Tours in New Hampshire

Old
Stage Rd.

NH 155

Mill Hill Rd.

Town
Hall Rd.

MADBURY

Madbury
Rose Farm

Start

UNH parking lot

NH 155A
Mast Rd.

US 4

Madbury Rd.

US 4

NH
155A →

Main St.

Edgewood Rd.
DURHAM

DOVER
inset

Ham St.

Central
Ave.
Chestnut
St.

Broadway

NH 4

Gulf
Rd.

Sixth St.

Cocheco
Rd.

Central Ave.
(NH 9/4/16)

NH 4

Spaulding
Tpk.

Silver
St.

Rutland
St.

NH 9/4

NH 9/16

NH 155

balloons, prevailing winds cooperating (332-9289).

Accommodations are plentiful. The New England Center in Durham, affiliated with the university's hotel management course, offers lodging and a prize-winning restaurant where the program's students strut their stuff with magnificent lunches, dinners, and Sunday brunches. For bed-and-breakfast devotees, Dover offers the Highland Farm, a large brick Victorian home amid rolling fields and nature trails along the Cocheco River near 22.1 miles of your ride (743-3399), and Pinky's Place, another Victorian home at 38 Rutland Street, just off Silver Street, a part of the route (742-8789). An institution of an eatery is Newick's Lobster House on Dover Point Road in Dover, serving volumes of seafood at rock-bottom prices. For lodging and dining closer to the ocean, see the accommodations under the Portsmouth-Little Boars Head tour (Tour 18).

The roads on this trip through the cradle of New Hampshire are remarkably uniform, with some exceptions at specific points in the ride descriptions. This summarizes the route: the terrain is flat to gently rolling with the numbered roads open and smooth with moderate traffic, good visibility, and excellent wide-paved shoulders. The smaller lanes are more winding and shaded, with little traffic and most stretches recently surfaced.

Start your ride at the University of New Hampshire parking lot, where Mast Road joins Main Street opposite the UNH fieldhouse, properly called the Lundholm Gymnasium.

0.0   From the parking lot turn left onto Main Street and ride 0.3 mile to Edgewood Road.

0.3   Turn left on Edgewood Road and ride 0.5 mile to Madbury Road (unmarked).

0.8   At the stop sign at Madbury Road turn left and ride 1.6 miles to NH 155. Stay on Madbury Road as it crosses US 4 at 1.5 miles.

2.4   At NH 155 North, turn right toward Dover and ride 2.8 miles to where NH 155 merges with NH 9.

The Madbury Rose Farm greenhouses described earlier are at this junction. If you don't want to stop now, keep riding because the ride returns past this corner.

5.2   As NH 155 merges with NH 9 East go straight and ride 1.1 miles. The road becomes Silver Street closer to downtown Dover.

Pinky's Place bed and breakfast, described earlier, is on Rutland Street, to the left off Silver Street.

6.3   At the traffic light opposite the Gulf service station, turn left on Central Avenue and follow NH 9/NH 16/NH 4 for 0.6 mile.

The Dover Municipal Building is at 6.6 miles on the left, and on the

Photo by Laura Scheibel

The Hamilton House gardens on the Maine side of the bi-state tour.

right is *Foster's Daily Democrat,* a newspaper named after its publishers.

6.9 **Stay with NH 4 and as the other numbered roads veer off uphill to the left, take the middle road (Portland Street) and ride 0.1 mile.**

7.0 **Bear right and ride 0.8 mile on Cocheco Road until it joins Gulf Road.**

7.8 **Bear right at the T-junction triangle onto Gulf Road for the 1.9-mile stretch into Maine.**

9.7 **Cross the Salmon Falls River into Maine, where the road becomes ME 101 (unmarked).**

10.0 **Take the first left, Waterside Road (unmarked) after you've crossed the New Hampshire-Maine bridge and ride for 0.5 mile to Oldfields Road.**

10.5 **At the T-junction and stop sign turn left onto Oldfields Road (unmarked) and follow it 2.8 miles into South Berwick, where it becomes Brattle Street shortly before the junction of ME 236.**
The Vaughan Woods Memorial, a 30-acre woodland state park along the Salmon Falls River offering hiking, picnicking, and toilets, is at 12.2 miles on the left. The handsome Hamilton House, c.1785, a Georgian mansion, is on the right at 12.4 miles. An abandoned woolen mill on the Great Works River at the bridge by Pine Street just before ME 236 testifies to the community's industrial past.
Oldfields is a flat rural road with a less-than-smooth surface, no shoulder, and very little traffic.

13.3 **Turn left at the T-junction of ME 236 and glide down 1 mile toward ME 4 in South Berwick.**

14.3 **At the T-junction of ME 4 go right for 0.5 mile to Main Street.**
The robust but stately First Baptist Church has guarded this junction since 1823.

14.8 **Bear left onto Main Street at the fork by the Getty service station and ride 0.3 mile toward the Salmon Falls River.**
At 15.0 miles you pass Fogarty's ice cream stand on the left.

15.1 **Cross the Salmon Falls River back into New Hampshire at Rollinsford, where the street becomes Front Street. Follow the road for 0.1 mile to Main Street.**
This tiny neighborhood of handsome well-preserved red-brick factory buildings, with a bit of imagination, becomes an accurate picture of a nineteenth-century mill community that Rollinsford's older residents still call "The Mill" or "The Village."

15.2 **Turn right onto Main Street and, keeping the railroad tracks to your right, go 1.1 miles to the Rollinsford Fire Department.**
In these few blocks you pass the Rollinsford Post Office, the Police Department, housed in a dignified towered white structure erected in 1893, and Giroux Market for snacks.

16.3 **At the fire station by the cemetery and Civil War monument with two cannons, bear left and for 0.5 mile follow the signs to Somersworth and Dover, while an overpass takes you over the railroad tracks you had been following.**

16.8 **At the fork, bear left, following the sign to Dover along Rollins Road (unmarked) for 0.4 mile.**

17.2 **Turn left at the T-junction and ride for 2.1 miles to Ham Street, following the road (which remains Rollins) into Dover where the street becomes Broadway (also unmarked).**

19.3 **Turn right onto Ham Street and ride 0.2 mile to Central Avenue.**

19.5 **At the stop sign turn left onto Central Avenue and ride 0.2 mile.**
If you're inexperienced or uncomfortable with city traffic, you may choose to walk your bicycle across.

19.7 **Bear right on Chestnut Street, then make an immediate right turn on Sixth Street (unmarked) opposite a florist and video shop and ride for 2.4 miles to County Farm Road.**

22.1 **Turn left on County Farm Road by a sign directing you to Strafford County institutions, ranging from the jail to the court and nursing home, and ride 0.3 mile.**
The Highland Farm bed and breakfast is on the left on County Farm Road, 0.3 mile beyond this turn.

22.4 **Turn left on Watson Road and ride 1 mile to Tolend Road (unmarked).**
You cross the Cocheco River just before you reach your next turn.

23.4 **At the T-junction with Tolend Road, turn right and pedal 0.6 mile to French Cross Road.**

24.0 **Turn left onto French Cross Road and ride 0.8 mile to NH 9.**

24.8 **Cross NH 9 (Littleworth Road). Once you're across, the road becomes Old Stage Road. Ride 0.4 mile to Mill Hill Road.**

25.2 **Mill Hill Road is your third right from where you crossed NH 9. Turn right and ride 1.3 mile to Town Hall Road.**

Photo by Tim Savard

A rest break on the New Hampshire-Maine tour.

26.5   Bear left on Town Hall Road and ride 0.9 mile to NH 155.

You pass the Congregational Church and Madbury Town Hall (1861).

27.4   Turn left onto NH 155 North, then immediately right onto Durham Road (unmarked) at the sign for the University of New Hampshire. Durham Road soon becomes Madbury Road (also unmarked). Ride 1.7 miles into Durham and Edgewood Road.

If you didn't visit the Madbury Rose Farm greenhouses at this junction near the start of this tour, now's the time.

29.1   Make a right onto Edgewood Road at the sign for the New England Center and ride 0.6 mile to Main Street.

29.7   At the Main Street T-junction, turn right and ride 0.3 mile to the parking lot.

To reward yourself before you reach the parking lot, bear right at the light after the turn onto Main Street and stop at the former Durham railroad station, now the University of New Hampshire Dairy Bar and Restaurant. It serves the best ice cream between Boston and Montreal, the product of the school's cows and agriculture students.

30.0   You're back where you began this two-state tour.

Bicycle Repair Services

Bicycle Bob's, 9 Government Street, Kittery, ME (9:30–6 Mon.–Wed., Fri.; 9:30–8 Thur.; 9:30–5 Sat.; 12–4 Sun) (207-439-3605)

Bikes 'N' Boards, 801 Islington Street, Portsmouth (9–6 Mon.–Thur.; 9–8 Fri.; 9–5 Sat.) (436-2453)

Durham Bike, Pette Brook Lane, Durham (9–6 Mon.–Fri.; 10–3 Sat.) (868-5634)

Peddler's Bicycle Shop, 1 Cate Street, Portsmouth (9–5:30 Tue.–Wed.; 9–8 Mon., Thur., Fri.; 9–5 Sat.) (436-0660)

Tony's Cyclery, 10 Fourth Street, Dover (9–5:30 Mon. Thur.; 9–7 Fri., 9–5 Sat.) (742-0494)

21

Exeter-Massachusetts

28.5 miles; easy cycling
Level to rolling terrain

Here, cycling across the gently rolling terrain of New Hampshire's coastal plain, you are free to absorb the vistas that unfold before you, for there are few hills and little traffic to distract you. A curve in the road may bring into view a tiny hamlet, an open expanse of pastureland, country-suburban residences, or the campus of one of America's most respected academies. Never strictly rural, this trip begins in the bustling town of Exeter not far from the buildings of famed Phillips Exeter Academy, then loops south through attractive countryside, dipping briefly into neighboring Massachusetts. It is hard to imagine that this region sits on the edge of a major urban complex, for although the deep woods and mountains that characterize so much of New Hampshire are missing, there is still much open farmland, and the newer homes are well spaced. Particularly appealing are the acres of apple orchards, with row upon row of trees brightly colored with blossoms in late spring and heavily laden with fruit in autumn. But whatever the season, the roads, towns, countryside, and terrain of this region combine to offer a pleasant day of easy riding.

Your trip starts at the foot of Front Street in the center of Exeter, by the town hall and bandstand. Parking is available here and throughout the town.

0.0 **From the bandstand, as you face the Ioka Theater movie house, turn right onto Water Street (NH 108). After 0.2 mile, NH 108 bears off to the left; your route continues straight on NH 27/NH 88 toward Hampton.**

Although Exeter's roots are firmly planted in its seventeenth-century past, its townsfolk have managed to accommodate twentieth-century demands while preserving many historical landmarks. Because of the many famous people in this town who left their mark, there are several significant historical sites to visit. If you have time to explore the town, pick up the booklet of walking tours printed by the Exeter Historical Society. You might take a tour of Phillips Exeter Academy, whose impact on the community has been considerable since its founding in 1781. Many of its buildings are open to the public.

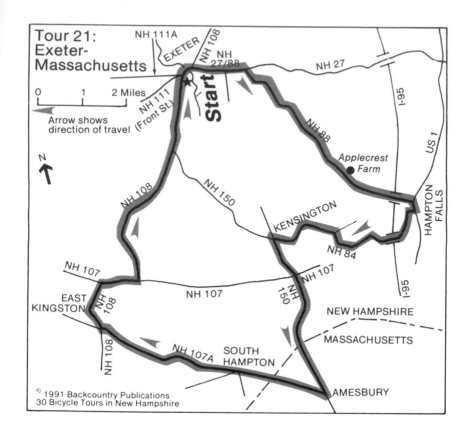

Lodging in Exeter is available at the Exeter Inn, 90 Front Street, on the Phillips Exeter Academy campus. It features Georgian architecture and a traditional dining room and cocktail lounge (772-5901). The Loaf and Ladle, 9 Water Street, offers informal dining, good food, and reasonable prices (11–8 daily except Sun., 778-8955). The Epicurean & Fox & Hounds Pub, 48 Portsmouth Avenue, features steaks, seafood, soups, and sandwiches, and quiche (lunch daily 11:30–4, dinner daily 5–9, 772-9300).

The route from Exeter to Hampton Falls is a winding country road. The surface is somewhat rough, but the roadway is level and bears little traffic.

1.3   **At the fork where NH 27 bears left to Hampton, bear right on NH 88 for 5.6 miles to a T-junction in Hampton Falls. (Do *not* miss this**

turn; but if you do, follow NH 27 for 5.6 miles, then take a right on US 1, and ride for 1.3 miles to the junction with NH 84 at Hampton Falls, described below at the 6.9-mile point.)

The 500-acre Applecrest Farm, 5.0 miles from Exeter, supports more than 20,000 apple trees, as well as smaller orchards of other fruit trees and some vegetable gardens. Fruit and produce, cider, maple syrup, home-baked breads and pastries, cheese, and other items are sold at the farm's roadside store, Applecrest Applemart, on NH 88. In season you may pick your own fruit if you wish. As you come into Hampton Falls, note the quaint Unitarian Meeting House and the Baptist Church, locally called the "Beer Bottle Church" because it is topped by a wooden copy of a beer bottle.

6.9   **At the junction in Hampton Falls, turn right onto US 1/NH 84 and then immediately right again onto the road signposted "Kensington." This is NH 84, which you follow for 4.3 miles to NH 150 on the outskirts of Kensington.**

NH 84 is a narrow, twisting, but level road. After taking you through a small residential area, it breaks into open countryside where there is little traffic.

11.2   **At the Kensington junction, turn sharply left onto NH 150, continue straight across NH 107, and ride for 3.9 miles over the state line and into thickly settled Amesbury, Massachusetts.**

NH 150 is wider than NH 84 and has gravel shoulders, good visibility, and light-to-moderate traffic. The terrain is more rolling than that over which you have just ridden.

15.1   **In Amesbury watch carefully for your next turn, because there are no town signs or route numbers to give you warning. As you come into the residential section of Amesbury on a slight down-grade, there will be a small triangular common with a granite war memorial. Here, make a hairpin right turn onto South Hampton Road, which becomes NH 107A as soon as it crosses the New Hampshire line. Continue on this road 6 miles, through South Hampton, to NH 108.**

This stretch of NH 107A is a two-lane road with no shoulder, light traffic, and good visibility. There is one gradual climb to South Hampton, which is followed by a downgrade. The rest of the route is quite level.

21.1   **At the junction, turn right onto NH 108 and ride 1.1 miles to the stop sign in East Kingston.**

22.2   **In East Kingston, turn right onto NH 107/NH 108 toward Exeter for 0.9 mile.**

Photo by Susan Heavey

Few hills, little traffic, and winding roads welcome the cyclist on the Exeter tour.

23.1 **At the fork where NH 107 continues straight, bear left to stay on NH 108, which brings you back to Exeter in 5.4 miles.**
NH 108 has a smooth surface, no shoulder, and moderate traffic. The terrain is level to rolling.

28.5 **At the yield sign in Exeter where NH 111 comes in from the left and NH 111A/NH 108 breaks off to the right, turn right onto Front Street to reach your point of departure.**

Bicycle Repair Services
Amesbury Skate & Sport Shop, 115 Main Street, Amesbury, MA (9–6 Mon.–Wed.; 9–8 Thur.–Sat.) (508-388-4544)
Exeter Cycles Bike Shop, 32 Portsmouth Avenue, Exeter (9:30–5:30 Mon.–Thurs.; 9:30–7 Fri.; 9–5 Sat.) (778-2331).
Gus' International Bicycle Shop, US 1, North Hampton (10–6 Mon.–Wed., Fri.; 10–8 Thur.; 10–5 Sat.) (964-5445)
Kingston Enterprises, 85 North Danville Road, off NH 125, Kingston (9–5 Tue.–Sat.) (642-3506)
Wheel Power, 37 Water Street, Exeter (9:30–5:30 Mon.–Sat.) (772-6343)

22

Portsmouth-Little Boars Head

33.0 miles; easy cycling
Level to slightly rolling terrain

New Hampshire has only 18 miles of Atlantic coastline, but that short distance makes up in variety what it lacks in length. Here you find pounding surf, fine sandy beaches, and rocky cliffs; salt marshes and small harbors; old forts and old villages. Because the sun and sea exert such a powerful attraction, you may encounter considerable traffic on this tour, especially on summer weekends. Consequently, we strongly suggest that you venture here only during mid-week in summer or preferably in late spring or early fall, when there is ample warmth, solitude, and space for an exhilarating ride.

Cruise along the winding road that parallels the shoreline and enjoy the great expanses of ocean views. On clear days, the Isle of Shoals lighthouse is visible more than 10 miles offshore, and you often can see freighters or sailing boats on the horizon. In addition to providing recreation, the ocean remains an avenue of travel, just as it was when early settlers found their way in 1623 to this shore's safe harbors. Much of the region's early history is preserved in numerous historical sites along the route, the most notable of which is Portsmouth's Strawbery Banke. This tour also takes you inland a short way through open, level farmland with weathered homes and barns. It is an ideal outing for those who wish to couple easy cycling with a generous diversity of potential activities.

There are many inns and lodges in the Portsmouth area. Several that you can try include: The Anchorage Motor Inn (431-8111), Howard Johnson's (436-7600), and The Port Motor Inn (436-4378), all near Exit 5 off I-95 at the Portsmouth Traffic Circle. The Inn at Christian Shore, 335 Maplewood Avenue (431-6770), is close to downtown.

Portsmouth is famous for its restaurants. One of the best known is the Blue Strawberry, 29 Ceres Street (431-6420), which features a six-course dinner. Reservations are required for this $38.00 feast. There are many other restaurants in the vicinity of Ceres and Bow Streets, including the Dolphin Striker, The Old Ferry Landing, and Poco Diablo for those who like Mexican food. For those who wish to combine cycling with other pleasurable activities, consider attending a play at the Ports-

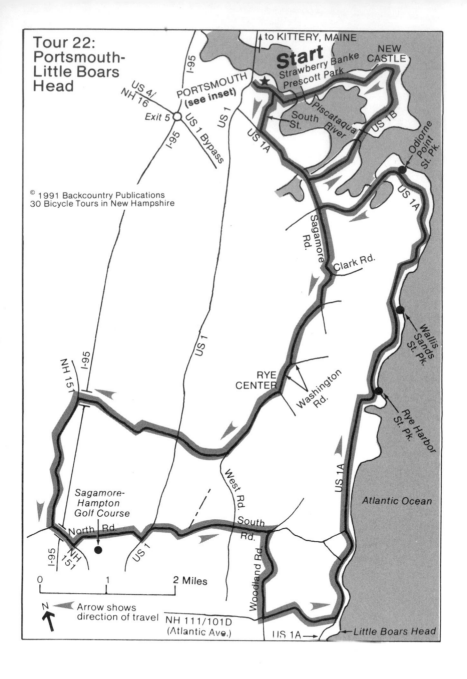

Tour 22:
Portsmouth–
Little Boars
Head

to KITTERY, MAINE

Start
Strawbery Banke
Prescott Park

NEW CASTLE

I-95

US 4/
NH 16

PORTSMOUTH
(see inset)

Exit 5

US 1 Bypass

US 1

US 1A

South St.

Piscataqua River

US 1B

Odiorne Point St. Pk.

US 1A

© 1991 Backcountry Publications
30 Bicycle Tours in New Hampshire

Sagamore Rd.

Clark Rd.

Wallis Sands St. Pk.

NH 151

I-95

US 1

RYE CENTER

Washington Rd.

US 1A

Rye Harbor St. Pk.

Atlantic Ocean

Sagamore-
Hampton
Golf Course

North Rd.

US 1

West Rd.

South Rd.

Woodland Rd.

I-95

NH 151

0   1   2 Miles

N

Arrow shows
direction of travel

NH 111/101D
(Atlantic Ave.)

US 1A

Little Boars Head

mouth Academy of Performing Arts, near the junction of US 1 and Bow Street (433-4472).

To reach the tour's start in the Strawbery Banke area of Portsmouth, follow the small strawberry signs along major routes into the city. Parking usually is available on side streets around the Banke, or in the municipal lot next to Prescott Park; the lot's entrance is by the corner of Marcy and State streets, adjacent to the old drawbridge to Kittery, Maine.

0.0 From the parking lot, turn left onto Marcy Street and cycle 0.4 mile to its end at a four-way intersection.

You pass the entrance to Strawbery Banke, a 10-acre museum with more than 30 buildings dating from the seventeenth, eighteenth, and nineteenth centuries. The grounds are open from May 1 to October 31. The lawns and gardens of Prescott Park, across the street from the Banke's entrance and stretching to the piers along the Piscataqua River, are the setting for an annual summer-long arts festival of plays and concerts, among other events.

Marcy Street is an old narrow, winding city street.

0.4 At the intersection, continue straight on South Street, passing the Olde Mill Fish Market on the left and following the signs to Hampton and Rye. Continue straight through to a traffic light at the junction of US 1A.

South Street is similar to Marcy, but slightly wider.

1.0 At the traffic light, turn left onto US 1A, also called Sagamore Road or Avenue, keeping the cemetery on your left. Continue for 1.6 miles, passing the intersection where US 1B leads left toward

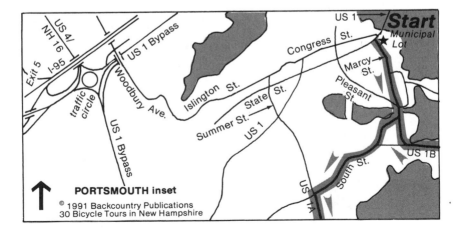

PORTSMOUTH inset
© 1991 Backcountry Publications
30 Bicycle Tours in New Hampshire

A bicyclist from a different age at Portsmouth's Strawbery Banke historical museum.

Courtesy Strawbery Banke

New Castle, to a four-way intersection with a blinking light, where US 1A curves sharply left.

US 1A is a wide two-lane road through a residential section of Portsmouth. While there may be substantial traffic, the speed limit is low. Ride as carefully here as you would in any city. Please note that the bridge just before the US 1B junction has open grates and should be walked over.

2.6 Where US 1A bears left toward Odiorne Point State Park (you will have a chance to explore the park and nature center on your return), continue on Sagamore Road toward Rye Center for 1.1 miles.

The roads between this junction and Little Boars Head (where you pick up US 1A again) are narrow with fair surfaces, no shoulders, good visibility, and little traffic. The terrain is generally level.

Foyes Corner Market at the junction of Sagamore Road and US 1A is open all day, every day.

3.7 Where Clark Road forks straight, curve right to stay on Sagamore Road for 0.5 mile.

4.2 At the next curve, bear right at the Mobil station on the road posted for Boston and Rye Center. Cycle for 1.1 miles.

5.3 Bear right on Washington Road and pass the Rye School.

A Cumberland Farms grocery is on the right where you join Washington Road.

5.6 In Rye Center, keep to the right of the war monument, following Washington Road toward US 1, Boston, and Manchester for 2.2 miles.

Time appears to have stood still in this part of Rye. Salt marshes, woods, and gardens stretch away from the many huge old homes that line the road you follow. In the center of the village, you can visit the burial ground from the Indian Massacre of 1691.

7.8 At the traffic light at the US 1 intersection, continue straight and follow the road 1.8 miles to a stop sign just beyond the I-95 overpass.

At 7.1 miles, on the corner of West Road and Sagamore, stands the Hitching Post Country Store, with crafts and collectibles (10–5 Mon.–Sat., noon–5 Sun.), and the Butt'ry Tea Room (10–5 Tues.–Sat., Sun. brunch 11–3, 964-8988).

9.6 At the stop sign, turn left onto NH 151 and cycle parallel to the interstate for 2.4 miles, this time passing over the superhighway.

12.0 Just beyond the overpass, turn left onto North Road, marked for

the Sagamore-Hampton Golf Course. Continue for 1.3 miles to a stop sign at the junction of US 1.

13.3   At the stop sign, turn left and then immediately right onto North Road (in Rye this road becomes South Road). Cycle along this road 1.9 miles to Woodland Road.

15.2   At this corner, turn right onto Woodland Road and ride for 1.5 miles to the stop sign at the junction of NH 111 (Atlantic Avenue).

16.7   At the junction of NH 111/Atlantic Avenue, turn left and head toward Little Boars Head, 1.2 miles away.

17.9   When you reach US 1A (Ocean Boulevard) at Little Boars Head, turn left for the 9.8-mile ride along the seashore.

Along US 1A, you pass numerous seaside mansions with sweeping lawns and rose gardens, and many smaller weathered structures with antique and craft shops. Rye Harbor State Park, jutting into the ocean, is an ideal spot for a picnic, lying 4 miles beyond Little Boars Head. Wallis Sands State Park, 2.2 miles beyond Rye Harbor, is a well-known swimming and sunning spot, while Odiorne Point State Park, 1.6 miles north of Wallis Sands, offers picnicking and hiking trails. It is also the site of Fort Dearborn, an Audubon Center, and the earliest (1623) English settlement in New Hampshire.

Along US 1A, numerous restaurants specialize in seafood and snacks. You can buy groceries all day, every day, at the Sandpiper Country Store and Coffee Shop, adjacent to the Dunes Motel, 2.4 miles from Little Boars Head, and at Philbrick's Store, 0.2 mile farther on.

US 1A along the Atlantic shoreline is narrow and winding, with intermittent shoulder. There are occasional paved walkways and a 0.9-mile bike path through Odiorne Point State Park. You will have to share the road with cars for much of this stretch and traffic can be heavy, especially on summer weekends, so use extreme caution if you cycle then.

27.7   When you reach the blinking light at the four-way intersection (through which you continued straight on your way to Rye Center), turn right to retrace your way on US 1A for 0.5 mile, as far as the US 1B cutoff to New Castle.

28.2   At the junction, turn right onto US 1B and follow this route 4.5 miles through New Castle back to Portsmouth.

On US 1B you pass Wentworth-by-the-Sea, under renovation, a reminder of the grandeur of late nineteenth-century hotels. New Castle, an island village dating back to 1623, is worth exploring. Its winding, narrow streets, Great Island Common, and the ruins of Fort Constitution combine to provide constant interest.

US 1B is, like US 1A, narrow and winding, but it carries less traffic. Use caution at the cross-grid bridge just before Wentworth-by-the-Sea and at the two bridges that bring you from Newcastle to Portsmouth. These last two have paved roadways but open-grate shoulders.

32.7   **When you return to the four-way intersection in Portsmouth by the Olde Mill Fish Market, turn right to retrace your route up Marcy Street to your start.**

33.0   **You are back at Prescott Park, where you began the tour.**

Bicycle Repair Services
Bicycle Bob's, 9 Government Street, Kittery ME (9:30–6:30 Mon.–Wed., Fri.;

The Portsmouth-Boars Head tour visits New Castle, settled in 1623.

Photo by David Brownell/NH Office of Vacation Travel

9:30–8 Thur.; 9:30–5 Sat.; 12–4 Sun., May–Sept) (207-439-3605).

Bikes 'n Boards, 801 Islington Street, Portsmouth (9–6 Mon.–Thur.; 9–8 Fri.; 9–5 Sat.) (436-2453)

Gus' International Bicycle Shop, Route 1, North Hampton (10–6 Mon.–Wed., Fri.; 10–8 Thur.; 10–5 Sat.) (964-5445).

Peddler's Bicycle Shop, 1 Cate Street, Portsmouth, (9–8 Mon., Thur., Fri.; 9–5:30 Tues.–Wed.; 9–5 Sat.) (436-0660)

23

Litchfield-Londonderry

17.5 miles; easy to moderate cycling
Level to rolling terrain

A green oasis surrounded by the state's major population centers, our Litchfield-Londonderry tour offers easy-to-moderate cycling, low traffic, and quick, easy access for most people in southern New Hampshire. Litchfield, a small community on the eastern bank of the Merrimack River, features basically level cycling and a nice warmup for later portions of the tour. Old farms with farm stands sell fresh vegetables and produce in season. Orchards invite the ambitious to "pick your own." The more heavily wooded town of Londonderry is hillier, with frequent but gentle undulations that contrast nicely with the open farms and floodplains of Litchfield. Londonderry was settled in 1718 by Scottish immigrants who came here via the Northern Ireland city of Londonderry, after which the New Hampshire town was named. Pockets of suburban development reflect population growth in southern New Hampshire but do not seriously detract from the quality of the experience. The town center, with churches, Grange, and green, is a pleasant reminder of bygone days.

To get to your starting point in Litchfield, take the Everett Turnpike to Exit 5 in Nashua. Follow NH 111 (Hollis Street) east for 2.7 miles to NH 3A, just across the Merrimack River in Hudson. Follow NH 3A north for 5.4 miles to its junction with Pinecrest Road. From Manchester, follow NH 3A (Brown Avenue) south from its junction with I-293 for 9 miles to the junction of Pinecrest Road.

0.0   Head north on NH 3A for 4.6 miles to its junction with Corning Road.

NH 3A is a level two-lane road with a double-yellow centerline and no shoulder. Because it connects Hudson and Manchester, traffic can be moderate to heavy during commuter hours. It is flat and reasonably straight, thereby affording reasonably good visibility for cyclist and driver.

At 0.6 mile, you will find the Litchfield Town Hall, fire department, and white-frame Presbyterian Church (founded 1809).

The McQuesten, Nanticook, and Durocher North farm stands

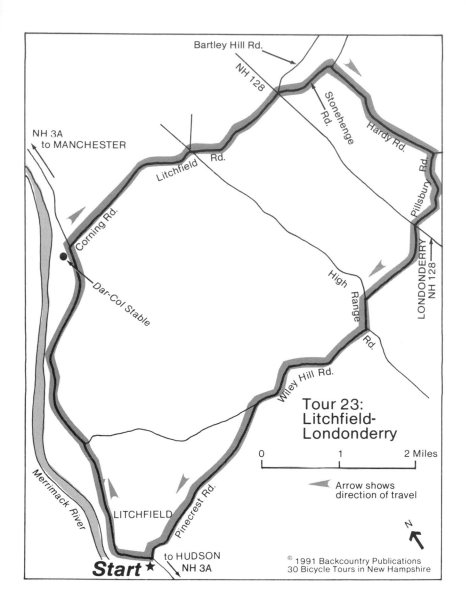

Bartley Hill Rd.

NH 128

Stonehenge Rd.

Hardy Rd.

Pillsbury Rd.

NH 3A
to MANCHESTER

Litchfield Rd.

Corning Rd.

Dar-Col Stable

LONDONDERRY
NH 128

High Range Rd.

Wiley Hill Rd.

Tour 23:
Litchfield-
Londonderry

0   1   2 Miles

Arrow shows
direction of travel

Merrimack River

LITCHFIELD

Pinecrest Rd.

N

Start ★   to HUDSON
NH 3A

© 1991 Backcountry Publications
30 Bicycle Tours in New Hampshire

are on the left at 1.6, 1.8, and 3.1 miles respectively. They are open only during the summer and early fall.

Litchfield Pizza is at 3.6 miles. Pantry Pride Convenience Mart is adjacent to Litchfield Pizza and is open all day, every day. Stock up for snacks or a picnic while in Litchfield, since there are no services on the rest of the tour.

4.6   Turn right onto Corning Road, which later becomes Litchfield Road, and ride 3.5 miles to its junction with NH 128.

Corning Road is located across the street from Dar-Col Stable, which offers riding lessons (424-3150).

Corning Road initially is a wide, flat, smoothly paved road that immediately goes through a small residential area. After 0.4 mile, the road narrows and the surroundings become more rural. At 0.6 mile, the road begins to ascend away from the Merrimack River. The road curves and rises, with occasional short descents, through old New England countryside to NH 128. The ascents, though frequent, are gentle and short.

8.1   Ride across NH 128 and immediately bear right at a fork onto Stonehenge Road (Do NOT bear left onto Bartley Hill Road) and ride 0.7 mile to the junction of Hardy Road.

Stonehenge Road ascends moderately, passing through a residential area, and becomes rural again. It is a typical New Hampshire backroad: narrow, no shoulder or centerline, and light traffic.

8.8   Turn right on Hardy Road and continue for 1.8 miles to a stop sign at the junction with Pillsbury Road.

Hardy Road is similar to Stonehenge Road. But the stone walls and trees that line the way make it a pleasant ride. You climb gradually for 0.7 mile to the entrance to Birchwood Ski Area, level out and descend all the way to Pillsbury Road. Beyond the ski area, the neighborhood turns more suburban.

10.6   Turn right on Pillsbury Road and ride one mile to its intersection with NH 128 in Londonderry, cross NH 128, and continue on Pillsbury Road for another 1.3 miles to its junction with High Range Road.

At the Pillsbury Road and NH 128 junction, the Londonderry Grange #44, Londonderry Presbyterian Church (built in 1837), United Methodist Church, and town green with war monument and bandstand offer a refreshing look at old New England.

A short descent down Pillsbury Road from NH 128 brings you to Mack's Apple Orchard, where you can "pick your own" in season.

Pillsbury Road, wider and smoother than Hardy Road, ascends gradually for 0.7 mile before a short descent to NH 128.

Courtesy Fred McLaughlin/Haggett's Bike Shop, Concord

Granite State Wheelmen signal a turn on the Litchfield-Londonderry tour.

12.9 **Turn left onto High Range Road and ride 0.3 mile to the junction of Wiley Hill Road on the right.**

13.2 **Turn right onto Wiley Hill Road and ride 1.9 miles to a fork, the junction of Hillcrest and Pinecrest roads.**

15.1 **Bear left on Pinecrest Road and ride 2.4 miles to its junction with NH 3A.**

Pillsbury, High Range and Pinecrest roads generally have the usual backroad characteristics—no shoulder or centerline, some frost heaves, and generally low traffic. The few short ascents repay with the more frequent and longer descents toward the Merrimack River and your starting point. Mostly rural, with trees frequently shading the road, this last section offers a pleasant end to your tour.

17.5 **You are back where you began.**

Bicycle Repair Services

Benson's Ski & Sports Shop, 6 Martin Street, Derry (7:30–8 Mon.–Fri.; 7:30–5 Sat.; 9–2 Sun.) (432-2531)

Bicycle World, 168-170 Rockingham Road, Londonderry (9:30–8 Tue.–Fri.; 9–5 Sat.) (437-3037)

Bike Barn Too, 14 East Broadway, Derry (9–5:30 Mon.–Fri.; 9–4 Sat.) (432-7907)

Merrimack Bicycle Shop, 1 Pinkerton Street, Derry (9:30–6 Mon., Tue., Sat.; 12–9 Thur., Fri.; closed Wed. and Sun.) (437-0277)

Lakes Region

24

Tamworth-North Sandwich

23.2 miles; moderate cycling
Rolling to hilly terrain; some short, steep hills

Between the White Mountain National Forest to the north and Lake Winnipesaukee to the south, this area in the foothills of the Presidential Range is surprisingly free of commercial recreation and development. For the cyclist, this happy circumstance offers a New Hampshire region whose inherent charm and beauty become apparent only upon close examination. If you are cycling in this area during the Columbus Day weekend and seek more gregarious diversion, try the Sandwich Fair, the least mercantile of the state's fairs.

Passing by farms, forests, and the tiny settlements of Wonalancet and Whittier in the town of Tamworth and a village in Sandwich, this tour has few commercial distractions to entice you off your bike, leaving you to negotiate the vicissitudes of backcountry roads. And while the tour covers enough distance and hills to make you know you've been cycling, it is a trip that will not leave you exhausted.

Two country inns are available near the tour's start. In Chocorua (pronounced *Shuh-CAR-oo-ah*), 2 miles east of the NH 113 and NH 113A junction, is Stafford's in the Field (323-7766), a 13-room inn set on a knoll and surrounded by acres of rolling fields. It offers a sedate setting and serves breakfast and dinner daily. The Tamworth Inn (323-7721), on Tamworth's main street, where you start this tour, is a 22-room nineteenth-century village inn. In addition to lodging, it offers dinner nightly 6–8:30 and Sunday brunch 11–2. The tavern is open until 1 AM with live entertainment weekends.

Your tour begins in the center of Tamworth by the inn, near the junction of NH 113 and NH 113A.

0.0   From the center of Tamworth, cycle 0.1 mile to the junction of NH 113 and NH 113A.

The Barnstormers Playhouse, across the street from the inn, houses New Hampshire's first summer theater. One of the nation's oldest, it was founded by Francis Grover Cleveland, son of the twenty-second president, in 1931. (President Cleveland was a famous summer resident of Tamworth; Mount Cleveland, in the Presidential Range,

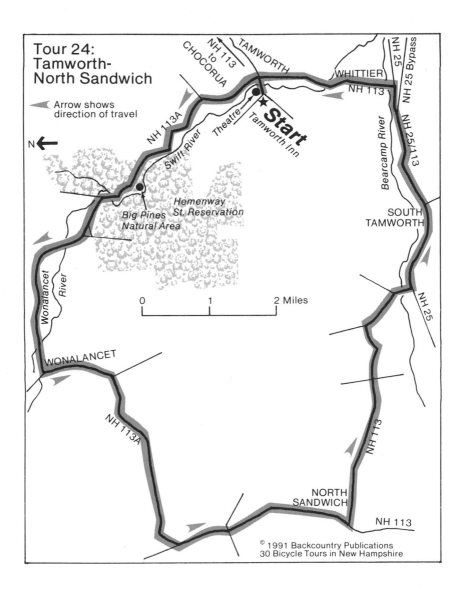

**Tour 24:
Tamworth-
North Sandwich**

◀ Arrow shows
direction of travel

N ◀

to NH 113
CHOCORUA
NH 113   TAMWORTH
WHITTIER
NH 113
NH 25
NH 25 Bypass

NH 113A
Swift River
Theatre
Tamworth Inn
★ **Start**

Bearcamp River
NH 25/113

Hemenway
St. Reservation

Big Pines
Natural Area

SOUTH
TAMWORTH

Wonalancet River

NH 25

0   1   2 Miles

WONALANCET

NH 113A

NH 113

NH 113

NORTH
SANDWICH

NH 113

© 1991 Backcountry Publications
30 Bicycle Tours in New Hampshire

bears his name). While the players used to travel an 80-mile weekly circuit, they now perform only at their Tamworth home.

Remick's Country Store in Tamworth is the only place to buy food until North Sandwich, about 14 miles away.

0.1   At the junction of numbered roads, turn left onto NH 113A West, heading north toward Wonalancet for 1 mile.

NH 113A takes you by the former site of the Chinook Kennels, which bred Alaskan malamute and Siberian husky sled dogs for show, racing, and exploration, including Richard Byrd's Antarctic expeditions and the army's search and rescue teams.

NH 113A is a winding roller-coaster road with a rough surface and no shoulder. Visibility generally is poor because of the dips and curves, but traffic is light.

1.1   When the road forks, stay left and head up a short hill, following the sign for NH 113A for 5.8 miles to Wonalancet.

The road follows the Swift and Wonalancet rivers to Wonalancet, named after the son of the great Penacook chief Passaconaway. Big Pines Natural Area, part of Hemenway State Forest, is on the left, 1.8 miles north of the fork, inviting a stop in the cool, shady woods.

6.9   In Wonalancet, follow NH 113A as it turns sharply left and ride 6.8 miles to NH 113 in North Sandwich.

The countryside is pleasant, with rolling farmland, stone fences, and stands of pine and birch, through which you get occasional glimpses of the nearby mountains.

This stretch of NH 113A is similar to the one over which you just cycled.

13.7   In North Sandwich, make a hairpin left turn onto NH 113 East at the sign for Tamworth and ride 4 miles to the T-junction with NH 25.

To divert from the route for food, the Old North Sandwich Store (8–7 Mon.–Sat., 9–5 Sun.) is in the village proper on NH 113A on the right, 0.2 mile after the junction with NH 113.

Road conditions are similar to those on NH 113A.

17.7   At the T-junction, turn left onto NH 25/NH 113 and ride 2.9 miles along the Bearcamp River through South Tamworth to Whittier, where the numbered roads split.

Whittier is named after the poet John Greenleaf Whittier, who summered in these hills. This stretch offers a variety of food. On the left, the Pastry Place is at 18.0 miles, and the Country Store is at 18.7 miles. On the right, Farm Made Ice Cream is at 18.9 miles, across the road from the Raspberry Bed and Breakfast.

NH 25 is a primary route, but this section is smooth, with a three-foot paved shoulder that disappears at narrow bridges. Traffic tends to be moderate, but the road is quite level with good visibility.

20.6   At the fork in Whittier, bear left on NH 113 East and ride 0.4 mile to where NH 113 makes a sharp left.

The Pioneer Restaurant and Snack Bar and Whittier Cash Market are on the right at 20.9 miles.

21.0   Turn left with NH 113 East as you cross the Bearcamp River and ride 2.1 miles to the junction with NH 113A in Tamworth.

Chequers Villa, an Italian-American restaurant and lounge, is on the left at 21.4 miles.

23.1   At the junction of NH 113 and NH 113A, turn left onto the main street of Tamworth and return to your point of embarkation.

23.2   The end.

Mountain vistas are just some of the many treats on the Tamworth–North Sandwich tour.

156 Tamworth–North Sandwich

Bicycle Repair Services

The Bike Shop, Mountain Valley Mall, North Conway (9–5:30 Mon.–Sat.; 12–4 Sun.) (356-6089)

Cycle Fix (bicycle road service) (569–8292)

Greasey Wheel, 40 South Main Street, Plymouth (10–6 daily, 10–8 Fri.) (536-3655)

Joe Jones Ski and Sport Shop, Main Street, North Conway (9–5 daily) (356–9411)

Nordic Skier Shop, Main and Mill Streets, Wolfeboro (9–6 Mon.–Sat.; 11–4 Sun.) (569-3151)

Piche's Ski & Sport Shop, Lehner Street, Wolfeboro (8–5:30 Mon.–Thur.; 8–8 Fri.; 8–5 Sat.; 10–5 Sun.) (569-8234)

Sports Outlet, Main Street, North Conway (9–6 daily) (356-3133)

25
Gilmanton Triangle

16.2 miles, moderate to difficult cycling
Hilly terrain

Collectively the setting for the 1950s-scandalous but now-tame novel and subsequent television soap opera *Peyton Place,* the three villages of Gilmanton Corner, Gilmanton Iron Works, and Lower Gilmanton form a triangle on the hilly western edge of the New Hampshire Lakes Region. Originally, the area was named Gilmanton after a large family, the Gilmans, many of whom received grants from Lieutenant-Governor John Wentworth of Massachusetts during his brief jurisdiction over New Hampshire. The Gilmantons were once much larger and were among the most populous towns in the state. Now they are quiet communities, removed from the more intense activity around Lakes Winnipesaukee, Winnisquam, and Squam. The three rural villages provide a beautiful setting for a short but hilly trip.

To lengthen your exploration of the Lakes Region, it is easy to connect this tour with Wolfeboro-Ossipee (Tour 26). Simply follow NH 140 northeast out of Gilmanton Iron Works (names for an ill-fated underwater iron-mining operation) for 6 miles to Alton. Then take NH 28 north into Alton Bay, where you can catch the M/S *Mount Washington* across Lake Winnipesaukee to Wolfeboro on Tuesdays, Thursdays, Saturdays, and Sundays at 10:15 AM and 1:30 PM from Memorial Day through October 21 (also at 4:45 PM from July 1 through Labor Day). Cost of the boat ride: $7.50 per person (366-5531 or 366-4837). Transport for bicycles is free.

To minimize the tour's ascents and maximize its descents, we calculated the ups and downs in both directions and found it only slightly more advantageous to ride the tour counterclockwise. The total descents are only 0.5 mile longer than the total ascents.

While there are no overnight accommodations within the Gilmantons, many surrounding towns such as Pittsfield, Alton, Gilford, and Laconia have motels and cottages.

Begin at the junction of NH 107 and Old Stage Road in Lower Gilmanton, 0.7 mile north of the junction of NH 129 and NH 107. Park alongside Old Stage Road.

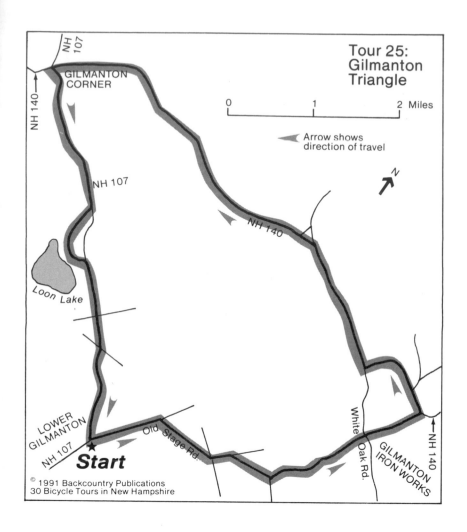

Tour 25:
Gilmanton
Triangle

0   1   2 Miles

Arrow shows
direction of travel

GILMANTON
CORNER

NH 107

NH 140

Loon Lake

LOWER
GILMANTON

NH 107

Old Stage Rd.

Start

White Oak Rd.

GILMANTON
IRON WORKS

NH 140

© 1991 Backcountry Publications
30 Bicycle Tours in New Hampshire

0.0   Follow Old Stage Road 4.6 miles to its junction with NH 140 in Gilmanton Iron Works.

Old Stage Road is a real New Hampshire backroad, recently re-paved. There is no shoulder or center line, and the frost heaves occasionally will send you airborne if you're not careful to ride around them. It offers some good views and about 3.6 miles of level and (sometimes steeply) descending terrain. Do not take any turns off Old Stage Road while it twists and turns toward Gilmanton Iron

Works. With the exception of White Oak Road on the right, 0.7 mile before Gilmanton Iron Works, any wrong turn will quickly turn to dirt. There are no facilities on this part of the tour.

4.6   In Gilmanton Iron Works, turn left onto NH 140 and continue for 6.7 miles into Gilmanton, sometimes called Gilmanton Corner.
The Village Store at the junction of Old Stage Road and NH 140 is a good place for lunch or a snack at a shaded picnic table. Open 9–7 every day, it has daily specials and a deli for fresh sandwiches. Some of the specials include fish chowder, beef stew, and chili ($1.50 per cup, $2.50 per bowl). Hamburgers and cheeseburgers are $1.50 and $1.75, respectively.

NH 140 is wide and smooth, with low-to-moderate traffic. It has

A quiet pastoral scene on the Gilmanton Triangle tour.

a paved shoulder for a short distance as you enter Gilmanton. Its gradual rises and dips all the way to Gilmanton make it a roller-coaster ride. With the exception of one long ascent of 1.3 miles, starting 2.4 miles from Gilmanton Iron Works, most of the ups and downs are 0.2 mile to 0.6 mile in length.

11.3 In Gilmanton turn left onto NH 107 and ride 4.9 miles back to your starting point at the junction of Old Stage Road and NH 107.

NH 107 is a two-lane road with smooth surface and no shoulder. Built in 1770, it was one of the earliest highways in New Hampshire and served as a supply route between the port of Durham and settlements in Coos County. Today this beautiful country road offers exceptional views of the Lakes Region. With the exception of one gradual ascent of 0.4 mile and a steep ascent of 0.8 mile, the terrain is level to descending all the way back to Old Stage Road. At 14.8 miles there is a breathtaking vista. Loon Lake Beach, for swimming, is at 13.8 miles, and "pick-your-own" blueberries are at 15.2 miles.

Big old homesteads with stone walls grace the main street of Gilmanton, as do the town library, Congregational Church, an old tavern (now a private residence), and the Gilmanton Academy Building. Founded in 1795 and graduating its last class in 1910, the academy was a highly regarded school that also had a theological seminary from 1846 until after the Civil War. On the National Register of Historic Sites, it was the village school until the 1940s and now is used for various town functions.

Gilmanton Corner Store, at the junction of NH 140 and NH 107 (7:30–7 Mon.–Sat., 7:30–6 Sun.), is a good place to buy food for lunch or a snack and enjoy the atmosphere of this picture-postcard New England setting.

16.2 Return to the junction of NH 107 and Old Stage Road.

Bicycle Repair Services

The Boot-N-Wheel, 368 Union Avenue, Laconia (8:30–5:30 Mon.–Thurs., Sat.; 8:30–9 Fri.) (524-7665)

Cycle Fix (bicycle road service) (569–8292)

Piche's Ski and Sport Shop, 318 Gilford Avenue, Gilford (8–5:30 Mon.–Fri.; 8–5 Sat.; 10–5 Sun.) (524-2068)

Truing Stand, 55 Elm Street, Laconia (9–6 Mon.–Wed., Fri.; 1–6 Thur.; 8–2 Sat.) (524-3687)

26
Wolfeboro-Ossipee

38.4 miles; moderate cycling
Some moderate to steep hills

Wolfeboro sits on the southeastern shore of Lake Winnipesaukee. New Hampshire's largest lake has 72 square miles of water surface, 283 miles of shoreline, and 274 habitable islands. John Wentworth, the last royal governor of New Hampshire, built a summer home on nearby Lake Wentworth in 1763, and as a result, the town became known as the "oldest summer resort in America." Living up to its name, the town has a very attractive Main Street overlooking Wolfeboro Bay and is a center of activity for the region, with a summer playhouse, golf course, many fine restaurants, and numerous overnight accommodations. Attractions such as the Wolfeboro Railroad and the M/S *Mount Washington* cruise ship, which stops in Wolfeboro every day, offer the opportunity for a noncycling view of New Hampshire's Lakes Region. Brewster Academy, a private coed boarding and day school for grades 9–12, overlooks the bay from its attractive campus near the junction of NH 28 and NH 109.

For the cyclist this trip offers the option of either a moderate day tour or a weekend/minivacation getaway. Once away from Wolfeboro, you will quickly find yourself in rolling countryside with frequent views of the region's numerous lakes, nicely maintained old houses, farm stands, occasional craft and antique shops, and enough small towns with stores and restaurants to keep you adequately stocked with food and drink. We do not recommend a loop along or around Lake Winnipesaukee, due to the potential for heavy traffic, especially on summer weekends, and the general lack of paved shoulder.

Ample lodging is available in and around Wolfeboro. But make advance reservations during the busy summer months. If you like the charm of old New England, consider the Wolfeboro Inn (569-3016), at the north end of town overlooking the lake. It offers bed-and-breakfast accommodations and has a restaurant and lounge as well.

Start at Wolfeboro Shopping Center on NH 109/NH 28 (Center Street), 0.2 mile from Main Street. Ample parking is available in this area.

0.0   From the Wolfeboro Shopping Center, turn left heading northeast on NH 109/NH 28 through Wolfeboro and Wolfeboro Falls for 3.1

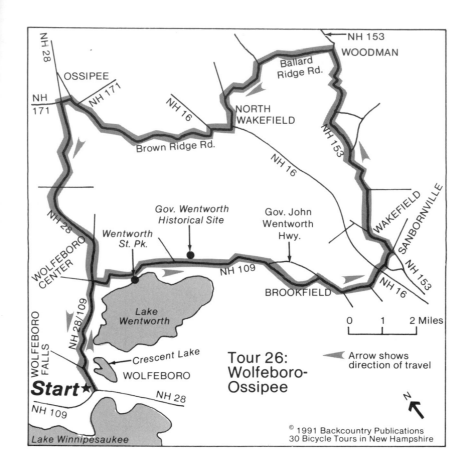

miles to Wolfeboro Center, where these two roads diverge.

NH 109/NH 28 is a two-lane road with a narrow paved shoulder varying in width from one to two feet. Traffic is generally light to moderate. The road rises gradually away from Lake Winnipesaukee. Good views of Crescent Lake can be seen at 1.4 miles.

Stores and restaurants abound in Wolfeboro. Several convenience stores, restaurants, and farm stands are available along the route for food and refreshment.

3.1 Turn right onto NH 109, heading toward Brookfield and Wakefield, and ride 9.2 miles to its junction with NH 16. Note a fork after 7.9

miles, where NH 109 bears left and the Governor John Wentworth Highway bears right. Stay to the left on NH 109.

A very scenic road, NH 109 is level as it hugs the Lake Wentworth shore for 2.5 miles. There is no shoulder, but traffic is usually light. After a gradual climb of 1.1 miles, the road rises and falls, gently but occasionally steeply, for the next 5.5 miles. These ascents and descents vary from 0.1 to 0.5 mile.

Wentworth State Park, adjacent to NH 109, 4.4 miles from your starting point, offers picnicking and swimming at Clow's Beach, a long sandy section of Lake Wentworth. The Governor John Wentworth Historic Site is at 5.8 miles. The tall pines surrounding the site make it a great place for picnics.

Fletcher Farm, at 7.8 miles, and Maynard's Farm Stand, at 11.9 miles, offer fresh fruits and vegetables in season.

12.3   Proceed across NH 16 and continue on NH 109 for 0.7 mile to the junction with NH 153.

Photo by Ken Williams/NH Office of Vacation Travel

Wolfboro–Ossipee tour begins in the nation's oldest summer resort.

13.0   Turn left and ride 1.1 miles to where NH 153 bears right. Follow NH 153 for 5.2 miles to its junction with Ballard Ridge Road in Woodman, a neighborhood of Wakefield.

NH 109 remains a two-lane road with no shoulder as it passes through a residential area and into the center of Sanbornville. NH 153 is a twisting, rolling road with a good surface, no shoulder, low-to-moderate traffic, and lots of picturesque views as it winds past numerous lakes and gentle hills.

Sanbornville is the southeastern terminus of the Wolfeboro Railroad, a tourist attraction that conducts rides to and from Wolfeboro daily, from mid-May to mid-October (569-4884). Several restaurants and food stores in town await, should you wish to take a lunch or snack break. Weathervane North, Wakefield Inn, and Sunnyside are right in town. Richard's Market is on NH 109, just beyond the railroad station and town hall. Poor People's Pub is at the junction of NH 109 and NH 153.

Lovell Brook Antiques (11–4:30 Sat.–Tues., and by appointment), specializing in old tools and furniture, is at the junction of NH 15 and NH 109. Westlook Yarn Craft (10–5 daily) is in Wakefield.

A and B Mini Market (8–after dark every day) and Seven Lakes Take Out are on NH 153, 3.5 miles from Sanbornville.

19.3   Turn left on Ballard Ridge Road (between two houses at the "Woodman N.H." sign) and ride 4.7 miles to its junction with NH 16 in North Wakefield.

Ballard Ridge Road is a typical New Hampshire backroad, with frost heaves, no shoulder, and no center line. After 0.3 mile, it begins a gradual rise for 0.5 mile and is steep for another 0.3 mile before leveling off at Twin Cedar Farm Stand. Thereafter, it descends, except for one short steep ascent, for 3.5 miles to NH 16, a wide, level, two-lane road with a paved shoulder that widens briefly to four lanes with shoulder near its junction with Brown Ridge Road.

24.0   Turn right onto NH 16 and continue for 0.6 mile to Brown Ridge Road, bearing left. Follow Brown Ridge Road for 4.7 miles to its junction with NH 171 in Ossipee.

The condition of Brown Ridge Road is similar to Ballard Ridge Road. After 0.5 mile, you climb a fairly steep hill for 0.5 mile. From this point the road has frequent, short ups and downs for 3.6 miles to Ossipee. Watch for railroad tracks at 27.2 miles. Lined with trees that form a shady canopy and well-kept old homes with fine views and stone walls, Brown Ridge Road offers a pleasant ride.

Moulton's Store (founded 1910) is in Ossipee near the junction of NH 171 and Brown Ridge Road (open daily).

M/S *Mount Washington* plies the waters of Lake Winnepesaukee.

29.3 **Bear left on NH 171, along the picturesque main street of Ossipee, riding past the Carroll County Courthouse and the Second Congregational Church for 0.3 mile to the junction with NH 28. Turn left and continue for 8.8 miles back to Wolfeboro.**

NH 28 is a two-lane road with a smooth, well-graded surface, long gradual ascents and descents, and a paved shoulder that varies in width from a full lane to one foot. The shoulder narrows significantly through Wolfeboro Falls and Wolfeboro.

38.4 **Return to Wolfeboro Shopping Center. Note that this tour can be reduced by 5.8 miles by beginning at the junction of NH 28 and NH 109 in Wolfeboro Center or at Wentworth State Park. The starting point in Wolfeboro was selected to incorporate a ride through the town at the beginning or end of the tour.**

Bicycle Repair Services

Cycle Fix (bicycle road service) (569–8292)

Nordic Skier Shop, Main and Mill Streets, Wolfeboro (9–6 Mon.–Sat.; 11–4 Sun.) (569-3151)

Piche's Ski & Sport Shop, Lehner Street, off Center Street, Wolfeboro (8–5:30 Mon.–Thur.; 8–8 Fri.; 8–5 Sat.; 10–5 Sun.) (569-8234)

North Country

27

North Conway-Bear Notch

36.8 miles; moderate to challenging cycling
Level to rolling terrain, many downgrades, and one long, gradual
climb

North Conway, the starting point for this trip, is a year-round resort community on US 302/NH 16 at the southeastern edge of the White Mountain National Forest. As the major gateway to the Presidential Range, it offers a variety of enticements to the tourist and outdoors lover, including shops, restaurants, and overnight accommodations. Our North Conway-Bear Notch tour offers an excellent opportunity to see by bicycle a particularly beautiful section of New Hampshire. The route involves only one long, gradual climb, through Bear Notch. The rest of the way winds along the Saco and Swift rivers through level-to-rolling terrain and includes lots of gentle downgrades to make cycling exhilarating and effortless. To put the icing on the cake, the road conditions are quite good, the traffic generally light, and the scenery spectacular.

There is plenty of lodging from Conway to Jackson. This region attracts tourists, especially in the summer and during foliage season. To ensure suitable accommodations, we suggest you take advantage of the free information and reservation service offered by the Mount Washington Valley Chamber of Commerce, Box 385, North Conway NH 03860. Call 356-3171 or stop by the booth on Main Street in the center of North Conway.

If you like little inns and guest houses, here are a few suggestions. Wild Flowers Guest House (356-2224) on NH 16, 1.5 miles north of North Conway village, is a charming 1879 house, complete with a woodstove in the parlor and a fireplace in the breakfast nook. We also recommend Sunny Side Inn (356-6239) on Seavey Street, a short walk or ride from downtown. Finally, the Center Chimney (356-6788) and the Nereledge Inn (356-2831) are both on River Road, within walking distance of town and on the route of your tour.

Among the many good places to eat is Horsefeathers (11:30–midnight daily) on Main Street (NH 16), a very popular pub/restaurant with great food. Around the corner on Seavey Street is Bellini's (11:30–11:30 daily), a similar type of place. For full-course dinners, the Red Parka Pub

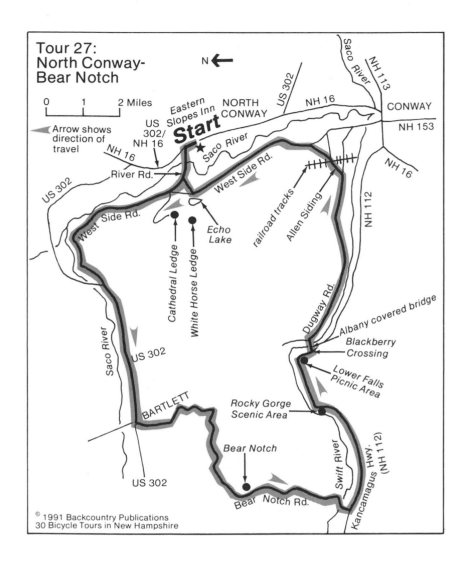

Tour 27:
North Conway-
Bear Notch

N ←

0   1   2 Miles

◄ Arrow shows
direction of
travel

© 1991 Backcountry Publications
30 Bicycle Tours in New Hampshire

(5–10 daily), at the junction of NH 16 and US 302 in Glen, is a good choice.

Your route begins at the north end of North Conway, near the Eastern Mountain Sports shop and Eastern Slopes Inn, where there is unmetered on-street parking.

0.0   Head north on US 302/NH 16 and ride for a very short distance to

River Road, on the left by the Gulf station and just beyond the Eastern Mountain Sports store.

US 302/NH 16 in North Conway is a busy road, where traffic is often heavy but slow moving.

0.1 At the intersection, turn left onto River Road, riding downhill under the railroad bridge toward the Saco River, which you cross in 1 mile.

River Road tends to be narrow with no shoulder.

Just past the railroad overpass at 0.2 mile are the Nereledge Inn and the Center Chimney Guest House, mentioned earlier.

1.1 Immediately after crossing the Saco River, River Road merges with West Side Road, from the left. Continue straight on this road for another 5.6 miles to US 302.

At the junction with West Side Road you clearly can see White Horse Ledge and Cathedral Ledge, two rock cliffs rising abruptly from the valley floor. In 0.5 mile you pass a paved access road to Cathedral Ledge; the climb to the top is challenging, but the view is outstanding. Foot trails also provide an easy hike to the top. Diana's Baths, a

Photo by Bill Johnson/NH Office of Vacation Travel

The Albany Bridge off the Kancamagus Highway leads onto a lightly traveled back road.

popular natural area with smooth rocks and refreshing pools, can be reached by trail from West Side Road, approximately 1 mile beyond the turnoff for Cathedral Ledge. A historical marker commemorating Lady Blanche, a noted writer and contributor to *Harper's* and the *Atlantic Monthly* who lived in a nearby cottage, is on the right, 0.7 mile beyond the trail to Diana's Bath.

This stretch of road also tends to be narrow with no shoulder. The visibility is generally good although sections curve enough to restrict your vision. Traffic is unpredictable in this area, but this road certainly is less traveled than US 302/NH 16.

6.7 **At the intersection with US 302, turn left and ride for 4.1 miles to the blinking light in Bartlett, just beyond the Bartlett Hotel.**

Several restaurants and food stores stand along the section of US 302 you travel and in the village of Bartlett.

US 302 is a wide two-lane road with a recently paved smooth surface, intermittent shoulder, and excellent visibility. It is one of the three major roads through the White Mountains, with heavy traffic. Because of its width and good visibility it can be ridden safely by the competent cyclist. But be careful.

10.8 **At the blinking light in Bartlett, turn left onto Bear Notch Road.**

David's Corner Store (open all day, every day) is at the junction of US 302 and Bear Notch Road.

Several turnoffs along Bear Notch Road offer excellent views of the Presidential Range.

Bear Notch Road is a forest highway with light traffic. It is wide and has been graded nicely to provide a smooth, gradual rise over the 4.1-mile ascent to Bear Notch. Once over the crest, you have a 5.0 mile downgrade to NH 112, the Kancamagus Highway.

19.9 **At the T-junction, turn left onto the Kancamagus Highway and ride 6.0 miles to the covered bridge at Blackberry Crossing.**

Be sure to stop at the Rocky Gorge Scenic Area, on the left, 3.5 miles beyond the junction of Bear Notch Road, and at Lower Falls Scenic Area, also on the left 2 miles beyond Rocky Gorge. Both offer opportunities to swim in the clear, rushing waters of the Swift River and to picnic by the waterfalls.

The Kancamagus Highway has a smooth surface and much traffic, especially on weekends. Although visibility is excellent and traffic tends to be slow, we urge caution.

25.9 **At Blackberry Crossing, turn left onto Dugway Road and immediately cross the Swift River through the covered bridge. Take an immediate right on the far side of the bridge and ride for 6.1 miles to Allen Siding.**

The Albany covered bridge was built in 1859.

From Blackberry Crossing to Allen Siding, the road is a narrow country byway, with some frost heaves, no shoulder, and lots of dips, rises, and curves. While visibility is restricted and road conditions are poor, traffic is very light.

32.0 **At the junction of Allen Siding, turn left and cycle 0.2 mile to a railroad crossing.**

32.2 **Immediately after crossing railroad tracks, bear left on Allen Siding and ride 0.4 mile to West Side Road.**

32.6 **Turn left onto West Side Road and cycle 4.6 miles to River Road.**
West Side Road is quite level and smooth, but it lacks a shoulder. Traffic is light to moderate.

At 36.8 miles you pass Echo Lake State Park, which offers picnicking, hiking, and swimming.

37.2 **At the junction with River Road, turn right and cycle back to US 302/NH 16 and the start.**

38.3 **You are back by the Eastern Mountain Sports store in North Conway.**

Bicycle Repair Services
The Bike Shop, Mountain Valley Mall, North Conway (9–5:30 Mon.–Sat.; 12–4 Sun.) (356-6089)
Joe Jones Ski and Sport Shop, Main Street, North Conway (9–5 daily) (356-9411)
Sports Outlet, Main Street, North Conway (9–6 daily) (356-3133)

28
Sugar Hill

15.0 miles; moderate cycling
Level to rolling terrain, one long hill

Sugar Hill is a small, undeveloped resort town on the western slope of the White Mountains. Commanding exceptional views of the surrounding countryside, its name comes from the large grove of sugar maples in the area. Having seceded from the adjacent town of Lisbon in 1962, it is New Hampshire's youngest municipality.

We selected Sugar Hill as the focal point of this short trip because it couples scenic beauty with low traffic and avoids the commercial development that characterizes many other tourist "meccas" in the White Mountains. Although you can complete the loop easily in a morning or afternoon, if you bring a picnic lunch and the weather invites swimming, it also can be stretched out to a leisurely all-day affair. From a "laid-back" cyclist's point of view, the only drawback is the long (nearly five miles) gradual climb to Sugar Hill, but that comes in the middle of the tour after you have warmed up. It also means you can cap the tour with an equally long descent.

We suggest you start this trip in Lisbon, midway between Woodsville and Littleton on US 302/NH 10. While no lodging is available in Lisbon, several inns dot Sugar Hill, the midpoint of your trip. An alternative is to start this tour in Sugar Hill, and brave the long climb at the end of the day. The Homestead (823-5564 or 823-9577), located on NH 117, 1.1 miles east of its junction with Pearl Lake Road, has 17 rooms in two buildings, including seven with private bath, and serves breakfast daily. With commanding views of the White Mountains, its porch is indeed inviting after a day of cycling. Many travelers have enjoyed this inn over its 100-year history. If you turn right at the Homestead and ride another 0.4 mile, you will come to Sunset Hill House (823-5522), a 35-room inn that features equally spectacular views of the Franconia Range. Offering three meals a day in five dining rooms, a bar, lounge, swimming pool, whirlpool, and nine-hole golf course, it has just about every modern convenience.

When exploring Sugar Hill, site of America's first organized ski school, be sure to look up two of New Hampshire's gastronomic land-

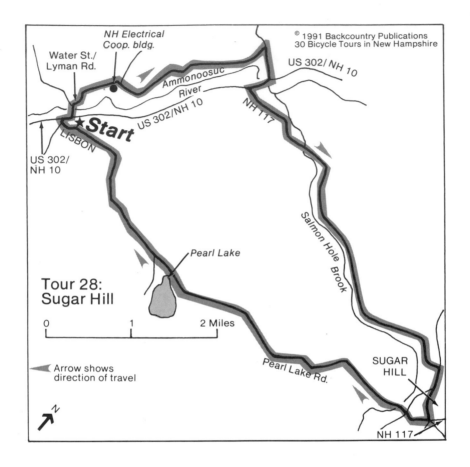

© 1991 Backcountry Publications
30 Bicycle Tours in New Hampshire

NH Electrical
Coop. bldg.

Water St./
Lyman Rd.

US 302/ NH 10

Ammonoosuc
River

US 302/NH 10

NH 117

★ Start

LISBON

US 302/
NH 10

Pearl Lake

Salmon Hole Brook

Tour 28:
Sugar Hill

0   1   2 Miles

◄ Arrow shows
direction of travel

Pearl Lake Rd.

SUGAR
HILL

NH 117

N

marks on NH 117. Polly's Pancake Parlor grinds its grains on its grounds for its blueberry, walnut, and coconut (among other flavors) pancakes and waffles, served with fresh fruit; Polly's stuffs its own sausage and compiles sandwiches of delights such as cob-smoked ham on home-baked bread. Harman's Country Store offers, according to some gourmet authorities, the finest cheddar cheeses in New England, procured from a secret source and aged twice and thrice as long as other cheese-makers consider adequate. The proprietors delight in discoursing on the proper preparation and presentation of cheese.

0.0   From the junction of US 302/NH 10 and School Street (unmarked but directly across the street from Northrop's IGA) in the center of town, head west on School Street, immediately crossing the Ammonoosuc River. Immediately beyond the bridge, by the Lisbon Town Hall, a large red Victorian structure, turn right onto Water Street/Lyman Road.

For more than 3 miles you'll parallel the meandering Ammonoosuc River through a narrow valley dotted with farm buildings and open fields.

Food is available at Northrup's IGA, directly across the street from your point of embarkation; Family's Roast Beef and Deli; Schatzi's Bakery and Cafe; and Chevallo's Pizza Plus—all on the main street.

The roads are narrow, with adequate surfaces over level-to-rolling terrain. While there is no shoulder, the traffic is very light.

0.8   Just beyond the New Hampshire Electrical Cooperative building, on the right, turn right onto an unmarked road and continue along the Ammonoosuc River for 2 miles to a junction with another unmarked road.

2.8   At the junction, turn right onto the unmarked road and ride 0.5 mile to US 302/NH 10.

3.3   At the junction, turn right onto the numbered highway, cross another bridge over the Ammonoosuc, and immediately turn left onto NH 117. You cycle up this road for 4.9 miles to reach the village of Sugar Hill.

NH 117 follows Salmon Hole Brook, reputed at one time to have had an inexhaustible supply of fish. True or not, the brook offers occasional opportunities to cool off on a hot summer day.

NH 117 is wider than the roads you have just traveled and has a smooth surface. Its shoulder is of variable quality; however, it provides a place to pull off if necessary. While you are climbing steadily toward Sugar Hill, the road visibility and the views of the countryside are magnificient. Traffic tends to be light.

8.2   Near the top of a hill, as the road veers left by a white house with a giant maple tree in the yard, make a hairpin right turn onto Pearl Lake Road (unmarked) and start a 6.7-mile descent back to Lisbon. Bear right when the road forks after 0.2 mile.

At this junction, NH 117 curves upward and to the left into Sugar Hill. If you can handle one more short ascent, follow it past the Pearl Lake Road turnoff through the center of the village and then turn around. You pass many pleasant homes, as well as the Sugar Hill Meeting House on the left, a structure built in 1830 and capped with

Stands of birch line Pearl Lake Road, your return route on the Sugar Hill tour.

a cupola and clock. The village also offers some spectacular views of the surrounding countryside, with the White Mountains as a backdrop.

Pearl Lake Road offers an exceptionally scenic ride past open fields and farms, alongside a stream and through stands of pine and birch. Pearl Lake, on your left, is a gem, with no development around it and no apparent restrictions on swimming.

The road is narrow and bumpy with no shoulder, little traffic, some steep downgrades, and occasional sharp curves. Be careful on the downgrades, because it is easy to get going too fast to negotiate some of the sharp curves safely.

14.9 **At the T-junction with Lisbon's main street, turn right and ride 0.1 mile back to the start.**

15.0 **You are back where you began.**

Bicycle Repair Services

Littleton Bicycle Shop, 6 Main Street, Littleton (9:30–5:30 Mon.–Thur.; 9:30–8 Fri.; 9:30–5 Sat.) (444-3437)

29

Dixville Notch Century

105.7 miles; very challenging cycling (one-day tour) or moderate to challenging cycling (two- or three-day tour)
Level to rolling terrain, one long climb, then rolling to hilly terrain

No book on cycle touring would be complete without a "century," or 100-mile ride, allowing the adventurous and experienced rider an opportunity to cover 100 or more miles in one day. We offer you two: this one, and the International Century ride (see Tour 30). Our Dixville Notch tour offers a superb challenge to a wide segment of the cycling population, because those who aren't up to century standards easily can convert this trip into a two- or three-day minivacation, using campsites or motels along the way.

With a mountain to cross and several hills to climb, the difficulty of this tour should not be underestimated. Much of the terrain, however, is level to gently rolling, through some of the most beautiful and remote sections of New Hampshire. If you elect to take it, you should be well equipped, have reasonable knowledge of bike maintenance, and carry a good toolkit, some spare parts, and emergency provisions in case you get stuck for the night.

This is not a trip that offers numerous alternative activities to complement your day of riding. You should love to ride, and be able to appreciate the wonders of northern New Hampshire's wilderness: the Androscoggin River, Dixville Notch with its sheer cliffs edged by pines and white birches, and the Connecticut River where it is still a narrow, meandering stream. Probably one of the most appealing aspects of the tour is the openness of the landscape. Our Dixville Notch tour tends to provide long sweeping views of the North Country.

This tour passes through cosmopolitan-sounding Berlin and Milan, the latter taking its name not from the Italian city but from Milan Harris, a prominent nineteenth-century New Hampshire industrialist. Berlin (pronounced *BURR-lin*) and Milan (pronounced *MY-lun*) are sustained by the natural resources of the area, the wild beauty that draws solace-seeking tourists, and the industrial contributions of the forests: timber, lumber, and pulp and paper manufacture.

The Traveler Motel (752-2500), 25 Pleasant Street (NH 16 South) at

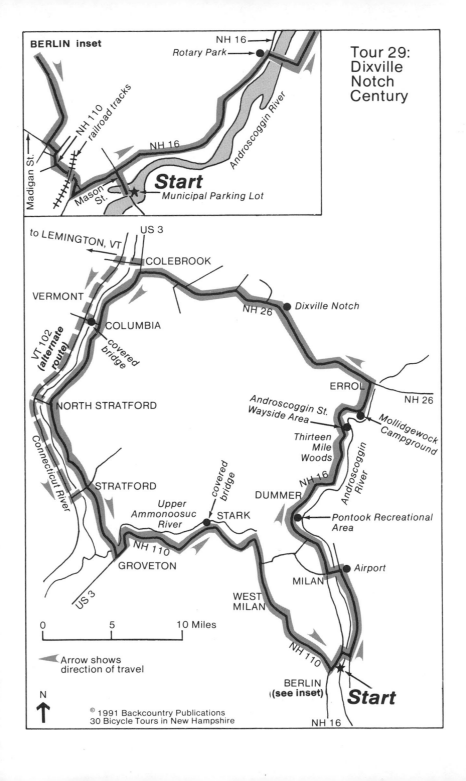

BERLIN inset

NH 16

Rotary Park

NH 110 railroad tracks

Madigan St.

Androscoggin River

NH 16

Mason St.

Start
Municipal Parking Lot

**Tour 29:
Dixville
Notch
Century**

to LEMINGTON, VT

US 3

COLEBROOK

VERMONT

NH 26

Dixville Notch

VT 102 (alternate route)

COLUMBIA

covered bridge

NORTH STRATFORD

ERROL

NH 26

*Androscoggin St.
Wayside Area*

*Mollidgewock
Campground*

Connecticut River

*Thirteen
Mile
Woods*

*Androscoggin
River*

STRATFORD

covered bridge

*Upper
Ammonoosuc
River*

STARK

NH 16

DUMMER

*Pontook Recreational
Area*

NH 110

GROVETON

Airport

US 3

MILAN

WEST
MILAN

NH 110

0   5   10 Miles

◄ Arrow shows
direction of travel

BERLIN
(see inset)

Start

N

© 1991 Backcountry Publications
30 Bicycle Tours in New Hampshire

NH 16

the south end of the city, is one of the few places to stay in Berlin. Other motels, inns, and campgrounds are mentioned as they occur along the route.

If you choose to sample a singularly grand part of this tour as a day trip—one of the most delightful in New Hampshire—you will have one of the easiest 34-mile rides in the state to refresh your soul. Start at 13.8 miles, at the Pontook Reservoir Recreation Area in Dummer (which has parking, public phones, and toilets), ride to mile 30.4 in Errol, and double back.

For the full tour, begin in Berlin at the municipal parking lot on Mason Street (unmarked), near the city hall. To get there, take NH 16 North, passing the Berlin City Bank on your left, to the traffic light by city hall and the Cumberland Farms store (6–midnight daily) to your right. Turn right at this light and go over a bridge. Before you reach a second bridge, you come to a free municipal parking lot. If you plan to make this more than a one-day trip, we suggest you notify Berlin Police that you are leaving your car overnight.

0.0 **From the parking lot, retrace your route to NH 16 by the city hall, turn right onto NH 16, and ride for 1.7 miles to a traffic light just beyond Rotary Park.**

There are numerous food stores and restaurants in Berlin, and we strongly urge you to stock up before you leave town. Once you are north of this city, there is only one store until Errol. Berlin Foodliner, on Pleasant Street adjacent to the Traveler Motel, is a large IGA, open every day 8 AM–9 PM daily, Sun. till 6 PM. There are several other variety stores between here and your turnoff near Rotary Park.

NH 16, from city hall to the traffic light by Rotary Park, offers poor riding through heavy traffic.

1.7 **At the light, turn right, crossing a new steel bridge over the Androscoggin River, and immediately bear left. Head north along the east bank of the river for 6.7 miles to Milan.**

The road on this side of the river generally is level with a smooth surface, little traffic, and fair visibility. The good shoulder disappears after 1.7 miles.

8.4 **By the sign for NH 16 in Milan, adjacent to the Berlin Municipal Airport, turn left and cycle 0.4 mile, crossing the Androscoggin again, to NH 16.**

As soon as you cross the river at the junction of NH 16, you will find the Milan Luncheonette and Variety Store, open all day, every day.

8.8 **At the junction with NH 16, turn right. Cycle north on NH 16 for 21.6 miles to Errol.**

This section of the trip is magnificently wild and beautiful, especially

Thirteen Mile Woods, a scenic preserve managed by the Boise Cascade Corporation, the James River Company, and the state. The preserve has no development of any kind. The road follows the west bank of the Androscoggin and offers endless spots to stop and comtemplate the wilderness—perhaps spot a family of loons. The Pontook Recreation Area in Dummer has public phone and toilets. The Androscoggin State Wayside Area, 16.8 miles north of Milan, has picnic tables and basic toilet facilities. The Androscoggin itself is a well-known and very popular river for canoeing, swimming, and fishing.

Camping is allowed by permit and only in one designated area, Mollidgewock Campground, 19.2 miles north of Milan. For information, call 482-3373.

Saco Bound, Box 119, Center Conway NH 03813, a canoe outfitting company, operates a whitewater school on the Androscoggin in Errol. For information, call 447-2177 or 447-3002.

From Milan to Errol, NH 16 has a smooth surface, little or no shoulder, excellent visibility, and, normally, light traffic. The terrain here is flat to gently rolling.

30.4 In Errol, turn left onto NH 26 for the 22.3-mile ride through Dixville Notch to the junction of US 3 in Colebrook.

With birch and fir trees growing out of sheer rock walls, Dixville Notch makes this climb worth the effort, especially after you cross the top. You are rewarded immediately with a view of the Balsams, a luxury resort often referred to as America's Switzerland because of

Jon-Pierre Lasseigne

A loon family sighted on the Dixville Notch Century route along the Androscoggin River in Errol.

its setting, architecture, and atmosphere.

Accommodations along this stretch are available at the Errol Motel (482-3256), located on NH 26, 0.3 mile east of its junction with NH 16; Log Haven Cabins and Camping Area (482-3294 or 482-3381), 7 miles west of Errol on NH 26: the Balsams Grand Resort Hotel (255-3000), 4 miles farther on; and the Redwood Motel (237-8781), 6 miles east of Colebrook.

Food is available at Food Trade at the junction of NH 16 and NH 26 and at the Errol General Store and Post Office, on NH 26, 0.2 mile east of its junction with NH 16. The Errol Restaurant, next door to Food Trade, is open 4:30 AM–9 PM daily. Redwood Restaurant and Country Store (part of the Redwood Motel) is open 7–10 daily.

NH 26 is a wide road with a smooth surface, good visibility, little traffic, and generally very little shoulder. However, because it is a primary highway, traffic tends to move fast. The terrain is generally level to rolling through forest and farm country; the only significant climb is 1.7 miles up to Dixville Notch. West of the notch you enjoy a long, sinuous downgrade.

Dixville Notch is also on the political road map. During New Hampshire's presidential primaries and elections, residents stay up until midnight for the privilege of being the first town in the country to cast and count ballots and announce election results.

52.7 In Colebrook, turn left onto US 3 and ride for 26.9 miles along the Connecticut River to Groveton.

This route along the east side of the Connecticut River offers many good views of the river and adjacent Vermont. Note the historical marker 14.8 miles south of Colebrook recounting early log drives down the river. Just before you reach your turnoff in Groveton, you pass a covered bridge.

(For an even more rural alternative, ride on the western side of the Connecticut River, crossing at Colebrook into Lemington, Vermont, heading south on VT 102, and recrossing into New Hampshire over one of three spans. Look on the left for bridges to these New Hampshire communities—Columbia (covered bridge), North Stratford, and Stratford. Back in New Hampshire, head south on US 3 for Groveton.)

In Colebrook, accommodations are available at the Colebrook Country Club and Motel (237-5566), located on NH 26, 0.5 mile east of its junction with US 3: and at the Northern Comfort Motel (237-4440) located on US 3, 1.3 miles south of Colebrook.

The Wilderness Restaurant on US 3, just a few yards south of the NH 26/US 3 junction, is open all day, every day. Prescott Farms, a large supermarket, open all day, every day except Sunday, when it closes at 4, is 0.3 mile north on US 3 from its junction with NH 26.

South of Colebrook you can buy food on US 3 at McGadden's (6.6 miles from Colebrook), open all day, every day; Champagne's Grocery Store (12 miles from Colebrook) and Covill's Variety Store, both in North Stratford and both open all day, every day. Emerson's Country Store is also open all day, every day.

US 3 is the major road linking the southern half of the state with Canada. Consequently, it carries some fast traffic and has fairly consistent ups and downs. However, the road is quite wide, the surface smooth, the visibility good, with a good shoulder. Beyond North Stratford the shoulder disappears until the outskirts of Groveton.

Photo by Laura Dore/NH Office of Vacation Travel

A ride along the Dixville Century route.

79.6 **In Groveton, turn left onto NH 110 and ride 25 miles back to Berlin.**

The village of Stark, 7 miles east of Groveton on NH 110, offers one of the most widely photographed New Hampshire scenes: the Stark covered bridge and adjacent church, both set against a backdrop of sheer cliffs.

In Groveton food is available at McKenzie's Diner on US 3, just before the downtown area (5:30–8 Mon.–Sat., 6–2 Sun.). In downtown Groveton is the S&W Market (8–6 Mon.–Sat., 9–1 Sun.). Wrenco Mini Mart, at the junction of US 3 and NH 110, is open all day, every day. On NH 110 three stores are open all day, every day: Stark General Store, at 6.4 miles from the junction of US 3 and NH 110; West Milan Grocery, at 13.8 miles; and Ducky's Mini Mart, at 22.4 miles.

NH 110 offers a wide, smooth surface with a consistent paved shoulder. There are some long ascents and descents; however, they tend to be more gradual than those on US 3. Road visibility is excellent, traffic tends to be light, and the views are great. As you

Courtesy NH Office of Vacation Travel

About twenty miles from the end of the Dixville Notch Century, Stark also is a stop along the Grand Groveton Gambol in tour 30.

approach Berlin, though, the shoulder disappears, the traffic increases, and riding conditions become urban. The last stretch of NH 110 takes you through a heavy commercial and industrial area.

104.6 **At the traffic light, a sign points left toward NH 16. Turn left and ride one block to Madigan Street. Here, turn right and ride one block, then bear left and continue downhill past the Berlin Police Station and through the railroad underpass to the traffic light by Dunkin' Donuts. Turn right, cycle one block, and then turn left onto NH 16. Continue past the Berlin City Bank to the traffic light by city hall, where you turn right.**

105.7 **You are back at the parking lot where your trip began.**

Bicycle Repair Services

Colebrook Chainsaw, 172 Main Street, Colebrook (8–7 Mon.–Fri.; 8–3 Sat.) (237-8544)

Croteau and Son Bicycle Repair, 507 Main Street, Berlin (2–9 Mon.–Fri.) (752-4963)

Moriah Sports, 101 Main Street, Gorham (9–6 Mon.–Thur.; 9–7 Fri.; 9–5 Sat.) (466-2317)

Tobin's Bicycle, 129 Main Street, Lancaster (10–5 Mon.–Sat.) (788-3144)

30

Waumbek Weekend: Three Rides North of the Great Notches

The distance, difficulty and terrain are stated at the start of each ride's directions.

The area of New Hampshire described as "North of the Great Notches," above the Crawford and Pinkham passes in the Presidential Range, is hardly touched by tourists. Below the notches, upper eastern New Hampshire is busier and more tourist oriented; it draws crowds to its factory outlets and shopping malls. But this part of the state along the Connecticut River does not lure the crowds. With the exception of a few tourist establishments along US 2, the region's most alluring attractions are its serenity, its profound panoramas, its bicycling-friendly roads, and its friendly people.

Here, three hours-plus north of Boston, in the land the late Governor Sherman Adams dubbed "the true North Country," the soils and vegetation change dramatically from those of the more southerly regions. In this land of moose and deer, pines are fewer and spruce and fir are more frequent. The hardwoods—beech, birch, and maple—tend to be of the hardier boreal, northern lines, like its residents. This is the land whose people grew so impatient with the bickering over the border between the United States and Canada that they declared independence from both nations in 1832 and formed their own Indian Stream Republic, submitting to New Hampshire four years later and finally becoming recognized as United States territory in 1842. The flooding rivers—especially the Israel and Connecticut (the latter the Algonquin word for "place of the long river")—enrich the valleys, and cows dot the riverside pastures, much as they did in the nineteenth century, when the White Mountain school of painting drew artists to these idyllic "intervales" (a regional term for alluvial valleys along the banks of streams).

Today, this territory caters to those who seek the relatively sedate activities of canoeing, golfing, hiking, fishing, hunting, tennis, and seasonal theater. In winter, visitors seek out cross-country skiing, snowshoeing, skating, backwoods snowmobiling, and the solitude of ice fishing. The visitor must drive away from this neighborhood of the White Mountains for the glitzier activities associated with Alpine skiing.

Photo by Jon-Pierre Lasseigne

A chapel in a mountain valley of uppermost New Hampshire, the land "north of the Great Notches."

We have savored and saved these three rides, new to this edition of the book, for the book's end — leaving the best for last. The White Mountains Meander, the Grand Groveton Gambol, and the International Century are "secret" rides, tucked away along Vermont's side of the Connecticut River and New Hampshire's eastern bank. They are known to relatively few bicyclists, who cherish them, but they are too magnificent not to be heralded and shared with all cyclists. Any one of them makes for a marvelous Waumbek Weekend of bicycling.

A delightfully surprising feature of these rides is that their terrain is remarkably flat. "North of the Notches" is a mountainous region, so a climb is occasionally necessary, but the routes generally follow streams in the intervales, making them less arduous than one would expect. The three rides range in length from 28 miles to 108 miles; and for truly bravura bicycling, the longest ride, International Century, can be stretched into a double-metric century, or 200 kilometers (128 miles).

Waumbek Weekend takes its name from 4,020-foot Mount Waumbek — and the Waumbek Inn at its foot. The Waumbek Inn (torn down in 1981) was among the few surviving nineteenth-century grand hotels in the White Mountains. In the shadow of Mount Washington—at 6,288 feet, the Northeast's highest peak—it once offered gracious hospitality and summer evenings of music by world-class performers under the moon and stars.

The inn also served as the headquarters for the Granite State Wheelmen's original International Century Weekend in 1979. Starting with a handful of riders, the International Century Weekend—called that because the main ride crosses into Canada—since has become an annual July event. The GSW celebrates the International Century rides with a distinctive insignia patch, showing a bicycle over the silhouette of New Hampshire, surrounded by the American stars and stripes, Canada's maple leaf, and Quebec's fleur-de-lis. These three rides, plus the longer Canadian double-metric century (an extension of the International Century ride), are the cream of the GSW's two dozen routes that yearly explore the North Country.

For accommodations, the region offers several bed-and-breakfast establishments. The Jefferson Inn, on the north side of US 2 in Jefferson near the junctions of NH 116 and NH 115A, is almost indispensable, especially for the longer rides. It is across the road from 2 previous starting points of the Waumbek rides, Jefferson's out-of-the-way, stream-fed public swimming hole. Offering the most imaginative breakfasts in the White Mountains (strawberry omelette popovers, for instance), the innkeepers also gather the guests in the Victorian common room for afternoon tea and freshly baked bounty (586-7998). If there's no room at the inn or if your group is too large for it, the Skywood Manor, on the south side of US 2 between the junctions of NH 116 and NH 115A (and another erstwhile GSW weekend headquarters), offers motel and inn rooms and swimming pool (586-4491). Camping is available on US 2 West toward Lancaster at Roger's Motel and Campground (788-4885) and at the Evergreen Motel and Campground (586-4449). For something more rustically exotic, Stag Hollow Inn and Llama Keep (no smoking), on NH 115 one mile south of US 2 on the left along the Israel River, provides not only bed and breakfast but adventures in the mountains and South American llamas to carry your gear.

If you decide to postpone the longer rides into Quebec, the Stark Village Inn is located halfway along the 58-mile Grand Groveton Gambol on NH 110, about seven miles from US 3 in Groveton. In picture-postcard Stark, population 518, at the end of a 151-foot twin-span covered bridge, this bed and breakfast welcomes you on the north side of the spectacular Upper Ammonoosuc River, and you can launch your canoe from the inn's doorstep (636-2644).

For the northern reaches of the International Century ride, Maurice's Motel (802-266-3311) and the Northland Restaurant and Lounge (802-266-9974) across the street from each other on VT 114 in Canaan,

Vermont (on the other side of the Connecticut from West Stewartstown), are the most conveniently situated amenities. The Northland's food draws devotees from New Hampshire, Vermont, and Quebec. The Lake Wallace Motel (802-266-3452) is about five miles to the west on VT 114. All three rides start in Jefferson, located on US 2, seven miles southeast of Lancaster. At an altitude of 1,412 feet, Jefferson is one of the highest communities in the state and it is the perfect place to start a ride because in all directions, the roads go downhill! Originally called Dartmouth, the community was renamed after Thomas Jefferson in 1796 — four years before he became the nation's third president. In Jefferson, the village of Riverton is the birthplace of Thaddeus Lowe (1823–1913), an early aeronautical, atmospheric, and metallurgical scientist who directed a military balloon force for the Union during the Civil War.

For all three rides, start in the Perkins Roadside Rest Area. Go to the tiny parking lot with picnic tables on the south side of US 2, across the road from the Jefferson Inn. An international evergreen tree–picnic table sign indicates the spot. Within yards, three stores to the west on US 2 in Jefferson offer provisions — Del's Variety, at the junction of NH 116 (ask Del about his experiences in Alaska), the Blue Jay 24-Hour Shopper–Estey's Market and Delicatessen, and the Old Corner Store, at the junction of NH 115A.

White Mountains Meander

27.9 Miles; easy to moderate cycling
Flat to rolling terrain, with one earnest climb

This ride explores the region between the Pilot Range to the northwest and the Presidential Range to the east, offering wide mountain vistas, meadows, farms, forests, and lakes.

You can trim this ride by about 3 miles by turning left from the rest area, taking an immediate left on NH 115A South, and hooking up to NH 115 South at Jefferson Station. The surface of NH 115A is rougher, although it is less traveled than US 2 East.

0.0 **From the Perkins Roadside Rest Area turn right on US 2 East and ride 3.8 miles to NH 115.**

The US 2 East leg, at 3.2 miles on the left, passes the Pig's Whistle Restaurant, which serves some of the finest blueberry pancakes south of the 45th parallel. At 3.5 miles on the right you encounter Six Gun City, a cowboy-town tourist attraction with a splendid carriage museum.

US 2 is smooth, with little or no shoulder, moderate traffic and mostly a downhill glide.

3.8 **Turn right on 115 South toward Twin Mountain and Franconia Notch State Park and ride 8.0 miles.**

This is one of the most scenic parts of the ride. It is mostly downhill, but at 7.0 miles the road begins to ascend gradually for about 3 miles. At 7.9 miles a historical marker describes the spectacular 1885 two-mile Cherry Mountain landslide. At 9.8 miles, as the climb levels out, it is worth the time to absorb the majestic panorama at the scenic pullout.

NH 115 is freshly resurfaced, and the former ups and downs at the far end of this leg have been graded off to a gradual climb, with restful plateaus. The road is wide open, with excellent visibility, moderate traffic, and a lane-wide shoulder.

11.8 **Turn right onto Lennon Road and coast 1.8 miles to US 3.**

This road is the reward for the climb you just completed! The downhill is exuberant, over somewhat less-than-smooth surfaces on

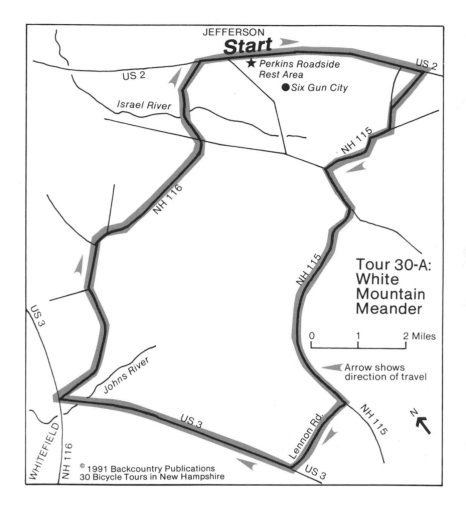

this shaded road. The wise cyclist will make ready use of the brakes
down this plunge.

**13.6 At the T-junction, turn right onto US 3 North and ride 4.7 miles into
Whitefield.**

Whitefield, population 1,900, has Colonial and Victorian structures
that surround the town common with bandstand. It is so typically
picture-postcard New England that it looks like a stage or movie set
for small-mountain-town Americana. The green has a tourist infor-

mation booth staffed with some of the friendliest volunteers this side of Mount Washington. The community has several restaurants and stores, an ice cream stand, and a pizza parlor.

The route toward Whitefield is splendidly scenic, with views of Mount Washington to the right, and there is an especially gorgeous sight of the 6,288-foot peak at 16.9 miles, as the road starts to descend into town. Be on the lookout for railroad tracks at 18.3 miles, just as the road levels off and merges with NH 115 on entering downtown.

US 3 is wide and generally flat, with surprisingly little traffic for a major road. It has excellent visibility and a shoulder.

18.3 After you cross the bridge over the Johns River into downtown Whitefield, ride 0.2 mile to NH 116 on the right.

18.5 Turn right onto NH 116 North and ride 8.9 miles to US 2 in Jefferson.

On the left just after the turn, you pass Sam's Supermarket, a good place to prepare yourself with full water bottle(s) because the ride to Jefferson is uphill. First it rises gradually, then at 22.0 miles it climbs steeply for 1 mile. Once the climb is behind you, the rest of the ride rolls up and down—mostly down—toward Jefferson.

NH 116 is smooth and properly shouldered, and has little traffic. It is intermittently shaded and open. The steepest climb is in the open and thus favors an overcast day. On a sunny, hot day remind yourself that the common sense of walking up hills carries no embarrassment.

27.4 At the T-junction, turn right onto US 2 East and ride 0.5 mile back to the start.

At this intersection, the owner of Del's Variety has built a combination gazebo-covered bridge-park bench over a tiny stream for a delightful rest stop.

US 2, for the next 0.5 mile back to the starting point, is smooth, with no shoulder, good visibility, and steady traffic in an area where three roads join. Ride cautiously.

27.9 You're back where you started, almost 28 miles ago.

Photo by Jon-Pierre Lasseigne

On the New Hampshire side of the Connecticut River in Columbia.

Grand Groveton Gambol

57.5 miles; easy to moderate cycling
Flat to rolling terrain, two climbs
Optional 8-mile shortcut

This ride makes for an invigorating one-day jaunt or a more relaxed two-day tour. The overnight stay coddles you in a bed and breakfast by a stream at the end of a covered bridge in the characteristically northern New England village of Stark. You ride through two covered bridges (or three or four bridges, if you make some slight detours), across and along the Connecticut and Upper Ammonoosuc rivers, to a magnificent picnic lunch stop on the common of Guildhall in Vermont. Vistas of meadows dotted with horses and cows and spectacular mountainous horizons greet you along backroads and little-traveled main highways. After a slow two-mile climb as the route ascends from Lost Nation, you are rewarded with a bracing three-mile plunge into Groveton. Starting with a downhill glide from the mountain community of Jefferson, the ride ends with a gradual climb of seven miles. That ascent sounds much worse than its reality and provides several bicycling-friendly, restful flat spots. You can cut about eight miles off this tour at the 43.1-mile point.

0.0   From the Perkins Roadside Rest Area turn left onto US 2 West and coast 0.7 miles to North Road on the right.
U.S. 2 has little or no shoulder, and moderate traffic for a major route, but it has good visibility and a silky-smooth surface.

0.7   Turn right onto North Road and ride 5.2 miles to Grange Road on the right.
North Road is a typical backwoods New Hampshire double-yellow line thoroughfare, generally smooth, with little traffic, no shoulder, and varying visibility. It takes you by open fields and forests that come to the edge of the lane. At 3.4 miles, you face a gradual 1-mile incline, but you are rewarded with a welcome truck-on-a-triangle sign that starts a 1.5-mile coast!

5.9   Turn right onto Grange Road and ride 11.2 miles to Groveton.
With its ups and downs, this section is as hilly as the ride gets. But it is well worth the effort, for you are compensated by majestic views

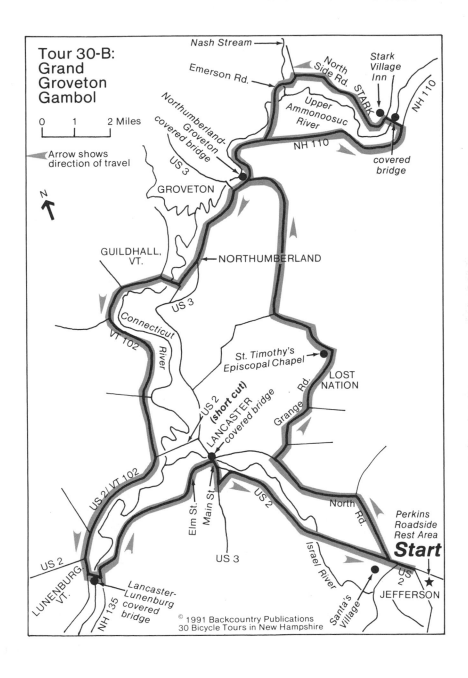

Tour 30-B:
Grand
Groveton
Gambol

0   1   2 Miles

Arrow shows
direction of travel

N

Nash Stream

Emerson Rd.

North Side Rd.   STARK

Stark Village Inn

NH 110

Northumberland-Groveton covered bridge

Upper Ammonoosuc River

US 3

GROVETON

NH 110

covered bridge

GUILDHALL, VT.

NORTHUMBERLAND

Connecticut River

VT 102

US 3

St. Timothy's Episcopal Chapel

LOST NATION

US 2 (short cut)

LANCASTER covered bridge

Grange Rd.

US 2/VT 102

Elm St.

Main St.

US 2

North Rd.

Perkins Roadside Rest Area

Start

US 2

JEFFERSON

US 2

LUNENBURG, VT.

NH 135

Lancaster-Lunenburg covered bridge

US 3

Israel River

Santa's Village

© 1991 Backcountry Publications
30 Bicycle Tours in New Hampshire

of mountains and meadows and streams as photogenic as a *National Geographic* travelogue. It takes you through a tiny community with the intriguing name of Lost Nation. White Mountain historians offer two accounts of the name's origin. One is that no road connected the community to its municipality of Northumberland, and thus it was a "lost nation." The other is that an itinerant preacher invoked the biblical allegory of a lost tribe or nation there.

The road makes a sharp left at 8.0 miles and takes you into Lost Nation, where at 9.6 miles you can't help but stop at St. Timothy's Episcopal Chapel, one of the most photogenic churches in the White Mountains. The road begins to rise gradually and then at about 12 miles climbs for 2 miles — with level respites, however. The reward is a bicyclist's gift: a 3-mile plunge into Groveton.

Grange Road is similar to North Road, but a bit narrower, with even less traffic and varying visibility.

17.1 **At the T-junction, turn right onto NH 110 East and travel 6.8 miles to Stark Village.**

At the junction, across NH 110 to your left, is the 136-foot Northumberland-Groveton covered bridge (1852), an appropriate spot for a picnic lunch.

This part of the tour follows the southern bank of the noble Upper Ammonoosuc River into tiny Stark, named after New Hampshire native John Stark, the general who led the victorious Revolutionary forces in the Battle of Bennington in 1777. During World War II, Stark was the site of New Hampshire's only prisoner-of-war camp, housing German and Austrian soldiers. In recent years, alumni of the camp and community of that time have begun to hold periodic reunions.

NH 110 is mostly flat, smooth, freshly surfaced, and open, with good visibility, moderate traffic, and shoulders that come and go.

23.9 **Turn left and go through the covered bridge.**

The Stark Village Inn sits at the north end of the bridge, built in the 1860s. The inn is a convenient place to spend the night if you're making this ride a two-day trip.

24.0 **Turn left onto North Side Road and ride 5.8 miles to NH 110.**

This road has two stretches of hard-packed dirt surface: at 25.1 miles and 26.9 miles. If you're bicycling here on the last Sunday in June, you'll find more-than-expected traffic on this rural road as music lovers converge on the annual International Fiddlers' Contest, held in a field on the left, just beyond the second stretch of dirt surface.

Be wary of railroad tracks at 24.5 miles. At 27.6 miles at the sign

Photo by Jon-Pierre Lasseigne

Resting along a Waumbek Weekend ride in northern New Hampshire.

for Groveton, the road takes a sharp left, becoming Emerson Road. It crosses Nash Stream at 28.2 miles and the Upper Ammonoosuc at 28.6 miles — both inviting swimming spots.

North Side Road/Emerson Road are rural byways with rough surfaces, good visibility, and very little traffic.

29.8   Turn right onto NH 110 West and ride 2.7 miles to US 3.

NH 110 is familiar because it brought you from Groveton to Stark.

32.5 **At the T-junction with US 3 turn left and ride 3.2 miles to Northumberland Village.**

Wrenco Minimart at this junction offers food. Provisions are available at several other points along US 3 South, including a shopping center and Dupuis Country Store, at 35.0 miles on the left.

US 3 is recently resurfaced and reshouldered, open, with good visibility and moderate traffic.

35.7 **Turn right at the white-on-green "Northumberland Village-Guildhall, Vt." sign and cross the railroad tracks and bridge into Guildhall.**

Guildhall (pronounced *GILL-hall*) is the Essex County seat on the western bank of the Connecticut River. Its green is surrounded by characteristic New England buildings, and it offers a serene spot to rest where two heroic oak trees shade a picnic table on the village common.

35.8 **Passing Guild Hall (the town hall) on your right, head south on VT 102 and ride 5.3 miles to where the road merges with US 2.**

This part of the ride, along the western bank of the Connecticut River, takes you past farms, meadows, an occasional field of barley or rye, cemeteries, forests, and McGrath's Antique Lamp Shop on your right.

VT 102 has an incline or two but is mostly flat, with a good surface, no shoulder, and very little traffic.

41.1 **Stay on the road as VT 102 merges with US 2, keeping the river to your left, and ride 3.9 miles.**

US 2 here crosses the Connecticut River to the left and offers a shortcut of about 8 miles back to Jefferson through Lancaster. If you elect to take this alternate route—which misses the Lancaster-Lunenburg covered bridge—follow US 2 East through Lancaster, then pick up directions at 50.5 miles below. You can make up for the missed bridge by exploring Lancaster and visiting its Mechanic Street covered bridge.

Traffic increases on US 2, a generally flat, smooth, wide-open road with good visibility and a two-foot shoulder.

45.0 **Where US 2 takes a sweeping right, turn up a steep hill, turn left on an unmarked road, and coast 0.5 mile to the covered bridge.**

The 260-foot, twin-span Lancaster-Lunenburg covered bridge was built in 1911 and reconstructed in 1983. Its eastern end has swimming access to the Connecticut River.

45.5 **Cross the bridge and, staying on the road, NH 135, ride 4.9 miles to Lancaster.**

This part of the tour, along the eastern bank of the Connecticut, presents several places to swim. The road travels past peaceful dairy farms and graceful New England houses.

NH 135, which becomes Elm Street as it nears the center of Lancaster, is a little-traveled backcountry road with a good surface and no shoulder. It is generally flat and has good visibility, with one incline for which you're paid back by a coast into town.

Lancaster, seat of Coos County (pronounced in two syllables: *COE-oss*), has several groceries, a supermarket, a bike shop, a movie theater, a weekly newspaper (the venerable Coos County Democrat), and several restaurants, including Olde Susannah's, a family style restaurant, and the classic art deco Lancaster Diner, both on Main Street; Carlos O'Brien's, a Mexican restaurant on Middle Street off Main; and Woodpile Inn, Continental style, on US 2 East toward Jefferson.

50.4 **In Lancaster, turn right where NH 135 (Elm Street) meets Main Street (US 2/US 3) and ride 0.1 mile to where US 2 and US 3 separate.**

50.5 **Bear right on US 3 and ride 0.1 mile to the top of a triangular green on your left.**

50.6 **Turn left after the Civil War memorial on the green, then make an immediate right turn onto US 2 East and ride 6.9 miles to Jefferson.**

You have begun your ascent back to Jefferson. The climb is kindly because it provides several restful respites of flat road. You pass the Woodpile Inn and the Roger's compound with water slide, motel, and campground on the right. The Woodpile Inn and Roger's are the current Granite State Wheelmen headquarters for the International Century Weekend in July.

At 58.3 miles on the right you pass another major tourist attraction of the region, Santa's Village, where your children will have a fine time. When the center of Jefferson with its solid white buildings comes into view, you are completing the climb.

US 2 is a major highway, with a smooth surface, moderate traffic, generally good visibility, and either a good shoulder or none at all, in about equal amounts between Lancaster and Jefferson.

57.5 **You're back at the Perkins Roadside Rest Area and the end of a magnificent ride!**

Bicycle Repair Services
Tobin's Bicycle, 129 Main Street, Lancaster (10–5 Mon.–Sat.) (788-3144)

International Century

108 miles; easy to moderate cycling
Flat to rolling terrain, two climbs
One voluntary elongation; four discretionary shortcuts

The centerpiece of the Waumbek Weekend, this route takes you from New Hampshire into both Vermont and Canada for an international ride, north along the eastern bank of the Connecticut River and back onto the western Vermont shore. It probably is the easiest "century," or 100-mile ride, in the region, and is positively the most pastorally picturesque. When this ride was inaugurated for the Granite State Wheelmen, one of your authors, Adolphe Bernotas, a GSW member, called it the "downhill century" because of its ease, saying that "a combination of geological, geographical and highway engineering vicissitudes make most of this outstanding ride downhill." Much good-natured ribbing was born of this description, which in truth is more factual than optimistic!

The ride starts at a high altitude and for the first fifty miles, with one exception, rolls downhill toward and along the Connecticut River. In New Hampshire, the road was built on the river valley hillside with fundamentally flat surfaces. On the return, the route follows the Vermont side of the river for 50 miles downstream and thus generally downhill to the Rogers' Rangers Bridge in Lancaster. Thus the first 100 miles generally glide downhill.

But the ride is a closed loop and must rise from Lancaster (altitude 864 feet) to the 1,412-foot elevation where it began. You have 7 miles to make up 548 feet. Even so, the final rise is mercifully mild; not a steady climb, the grades come in stages with restful plateaus and even one short, steep downhill to ease the ascent.

Another comfort of this ride is that it has four shortcut routes. As you ride along the river, several bridges can take you to the Vermont side for truncated return tours of 47, 64, 80, or 90 total miles.

A challenging feature allows you to achieve a "double-metric century," or 200 kilometers, by extending the ride into Canada. The ordinary cyclist averages 10 miles per hour, so cut yourself enough slack to return before dark. If you leave so early that breakfast isn't available in Jefferson, McKenzie's in Groveton is located strategically at 18 miles, the traditional breakfast stop of the Granite State Wheelmen for this ride. If you're making this a two-day adventure, make reservations at Maurice's Motel in Canaan, Vermont (802-266-3311), at 51.4 miles.

0.0 **From the Perkins Roadside Rest Area turn left onto US 2 West and coast 0.7 miles to North Road on the right.**

U.S. 2 has little or no shoulder, and moderate traffic for a major route, but good visibility and a silky-smooth surface.

0.7 **Turn right onto North Road and ride 5.2 miles to Grange Road on the right.**

North Road is a typical backwoods New Hampshire double-yellow-line thoroughfare, generally smooth, with little traffic, no shoulder, and varying visibility as it passes open fields and forests that come to the edge of the lane. At 3.4 miles, you face a gradual 1-mile incline, for which you are rewarded with a 1.5-mile coast.

5.9 **Turn right onto Grange Road and ride 11.2 miles to Groveton.**

This section is as hilly as the ride gets. But you are rewarded with majestic views of mountains and meadows, pastures and streams. The road makes a sharp left at 8.0 miles and takes you into Lost Nation where, at 9.6 miles, St. Timothy's Episcopal Chapel demands to be photographed. Here the road starts to ascend gradually and then at about 12 miles climbs for 2 miles—with level respites, however. The recompense is a 3-mile downhill into Groveton.

Grange Road is similar to North Road, but a bit narrower, with even less traffic and varying visibility.

17.1 **At the T-junction with NH 110 turn left and pedal either through the covered bridge or go to US 3, turn right, ride across the bridge, and continue for 34.0 miles to West Stewartstown.**

You pass through Groveton, a paper mill town that has at least three groceries: Wrenco Minimart at the NH 110/US 3 junction, the Groveton Market, and the S&W Supermarket, at 17.5 miles, across the street from each other on Main Street. If you want to breakfast on the finest muffins north of the Upper Ammonoosuc River, McKenzie's is at 18.0 miles on the left.

You also pass through Stratford, North Stratford, Columbia, and Colebrook. Each of these communities offers bridges to your left to cross into Vermont for shortened rides of 47, 64, 80 and 90 miles respectively.

Emerson's Country Store in Stratford on the left, at 26.2 miles; Stratford Truck Stop Mini Mart and Village Restaurant, on the right at 29.2 miles; Covill's Store, at 30.2 miles on the right; and McGadden's General Store on the right in North Stratford, at 36.7 miles, offer provisions.

You ride from panorama to panorama of pastoral scenes to

your left, along the serene Connecticut River. You pass by re-
minders of this area's livelier times, especially near North Stratford,
where on the left a historical marker at 29.4 miles recalls the exploits
of "White-water men," who risked life and limb to drive logs down the
river. Just beyond the marker on the left is a row of several identical
houses, recalling the era of company stores, even company houses
and towns.

Just before the Columbia-Colebrook town line, on the right at
41.8 miles, you pass the noteworthy Our Lady of Grace Roman
Catholic Shrine, oriented to the motorized. The stations of the cross
can be completed by car. This is a major attraction for motorcyclists,
who converge on the shrine for the blessing of their machines in
autumn.

Colebrook, population 2,400, is the largest community through
which you pass until Lancaster, 7 miles from the end of the tour. It
has a supermarket, several stores and restaurants, and New Hampshire's northernmost bicycle shop, at 43.1 miles on the left. If you
ask discreetly, townspeople will point out the defunct service station
where Florida serial killer Christopher Wilder met his end at the
hands of two New Hampshire state troopers on Friday, April 13,
1984. Past the center of town on the right, on a knoll overlooking the
expanse of the river valley, is one of the state's loveliest rest areas, at
45.7 miles. It offers cool clear water, a telephone, and a place for a
moment of repose.

For a major north-south highway, US 3 for the most part has

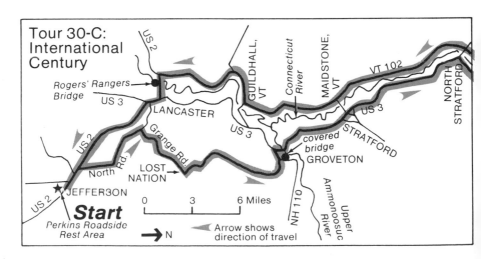

exceptionally light traffic. It has recently been resurfaced and is smooth. Most of it is open, with excellent visibility and shaded areas appropriately placed at the few inclines along this mostly downhill route. More than half of the road between Groteon and West Stewartstown has shoulders, varying in width from barely discernible to one lane wide.

51.1 **In West Stewartstown, just after a downhill, turn left on NH 114 at signs for Sherbrooke and Montreal and ride 0.3 mile across a steel bridge into Canaan, Vermont, and VT 253 on your right.**

You do not leave New Hampshire here until you are on the western side of the river. The border is the mean-water mark on the Vermont side, giving New Hampshire jurisdiction over the Connecticut River!

At least four places for food are found in the 0.3 mile between this turn and the next. The Spa Restaurant is on the left as you make the turn onto NH 114; Solomon's Supermarket, an abundantly supplied store, is on the right, just before the bridge; and just after the bridge on the right in Canaan, you'll find the Northland Restaurant and Lounge and Ray's Snack Bar. Across the street is Maurice's Motel, the overnight spot if you're making this a two-day event. If you're lunching al fresco or taking a break here, the West Stewartstown bandstand, across the street from Solomon's, or the green, across the street from the terminus of VT 253, are the places to go.

You'll be in Quebec soon after you cross the 45th parallel in Vermont—the halfway point between the North Pole and the Equa-

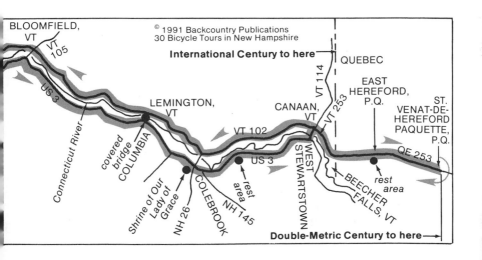

tor. You can get photographic proof that you stood at the center of the earth's North Temperate Zone by taking a picture at the marker on the left side of US 3 in New Hampshire, but you must ride 0.5 mile beyond the turn on NH 114, just north of the center of West Stewartstown.

51.4   Between the Gulf service station and Ray's Snack Bar, turn right on VT 253 and ride 1.9 miles to the blinking light in Beecher Falls.
Here is the fifth—heretofore unannounced—place to shorten your trip, if you really must. Go left on VT 102 and follow the directions from mile 55.8. But you are so close! Another 2.2 miles gets you to Canada, so you might as well go for it!

On your way to Beecher Falls, be wary of two unfortunately angled railway crossings.

VT 253 is little traveled, generally smooth, and flat, with no shoulder.

53.3   At the blinker at the sign for Canada, follow VT 253 North for 0.3 mile to the Canadian Customs building at East Hereford, Quebec.
Be careful of railroad tracks that lead to the Ethan Allen Furniture factory on the right, just a few yards before the border.

First, you will pass the U.S. Customs building, where you need not stop. You must stop at its Canadian counterpart, directly across the road from the "Bienvenue à Québec—Welcome to Quebec" sign, where tradition requires that you get photographed as proof of your international bike trek. This is the turnaround for the century ride, at 53.6 miles.

To ride the double-metric century, stay on QE 253 until you reach Saint Venat-de-Hereford Paquette. At 57.8 miles you pass a prize-winning rest area on your right, just before the village of East Hereford. You pass the Montagnard Motel on the right atop a hill at 58.7 miles. After an earnest climb, you take a left at 62.3 miles at the "Paquette" sign to the parking lot of the Notre Dame de La Confiance Church, which demands a visit. This is the turnaround, at 62.5 miles. Retrace your way for 8.9 miles to the Canada-U.S. border. On your return, for a delightful diversion just after the Montagnard Motel (which serves food), take a right on Rue de L'Eglise, loop through the village of East Hereford, and rejoin QE 253 South after taking a left on Rue Principale.

53.6   Retrace your way along VT 253 South to Canaan for 2.2 miles.
You must stop at U.S. Customs. Refrain from joking about contraband. The customs officers are pleasant and polite, but they turn unfriendly at jests about certain topics.

Photo by Jon-Pierre Lasseigne

An International Century rider at a geographic landmark in Stewartstown.

55.8 Cross VT 114 and head out on VT 102 South for 43.5 miles to US 2 in Guildhall.

This is the best part of the ride. You follow the meandering Connecticut downriver—thus gently downhill, with an occasional rise. You encounter few cars as you pedal past a covered bridge and villages so typically New England, they seem almost contrived. Increasingly spectacular panoramas of the fertile river valley constantly come into view on your left, against a backdrop of New Hampshire's mountains.

Make sure you're provisioned, especially with water, because the nearest store is almost 21 miles away. At 66.7 miles on the right, you pass the tiny, handsome Lemington Town Hall. At 67.1 on the left, you pass the 1912 Columbia covered bridge, the most northerly covered span across the Connecticut. At 85.9 miles on the right, a cold spring water pipe awaits your water bottle. De Banville's Store is at 76.5 miles, at the intersection of VT 102 and VT 105 in Bloomfield.

At 92.5 miles, VT 102 makes a sharp right turn in Guildhall (pronounced *GILL-hall*), just beyond the village common ringed by typical northern New England structures—church, parsonage, courthouse, town hall. If you need to rest, there is an idyllic spot in the shade of two majestic oaks. Chartered in 1761, Guildhall was the frontier during the French and Indian War, becoming the Essex county seat in 1802.

VT 102 has an incline or two, but the general grade is down as the road follows the river. Most of it is smooth and open to sublime views, with few meager stretches of shoulder. Traffic is almost absent.

99.3 Where VT 102 ends at US 2, turn left and ride across Rogers' Rangers Bridge into Lancaster for 0.9 mile.

The bridge was named after the militia led by Robert Rogers (1731–95), an American frontier soldier who distinguished himself in campaigns against the French over Lake George during the Seven Years' War.

100.2 As US 3 merges from the left with US 2 into Main Street, bear right and ride through Lancaster for 0.8 mile to where US 2 and US 3 diverge.

Lancaster, seat of Coos County (pronounced in two syllables: *COE-oss*) in late August is usually the site of one of the state's major fairs. It has several groceries, a supermarket, a bike shop, a movie theater, and several restaurants, including Olde Susannah's, family style; the Lancaster Diner; Carlos O'Brien's, for Mexican fare; and Woodpile Inn, for Continental cooking.

101.0 **Bear right on US 3 South and ride 0.1 mile to the top of a triangular green on your left.**

101.1 **Turn left after the Civil War memorial on the green, then make an immediate right turn on US 2 East and ride 6.9 miles to Jefferson.**
The climb back to Jefferson provides many flat areas to recoup from the inclines. You pass the Woodpile Inn and Roger's compound, with motel, water slide, and campground on the right. At 58.3 miles on the right is Santa's Village, a major tourist draw. As Jefferson's white buildings come into view, the climb is almost over.

US 2 is a major highway, with moderate traffic, generally good visibility, a smooth surface, and either a fine shoulder or none, in about equal parts between Lancaster and Jefferson.

108.0 **You're back at the Perkins Roadside Rest Area, with a century to remember!**

Bicycle Repair Services
Colebrook Chainsaw, 172 Main Street, Colebrook (8–7 Mon.–Fri.; 8–3 Sat.) (237–8544)
Tobin's Bicycle, 129 Main Street, Lancaster (10–5 Mon.–Sat.) (788-3144)